FROM RURIK TO PETER THE GREAT

Histor   istory, in the words of Edmond Goncourt, is a novel that was in reality. Such is the history of Russia – sometimes dramatic, sometimes terrible and sometimes not quite clear. The main characters on many of its early pages belong to the two dynasties – the Rurik and the Romanov dynasties.

"In the year 862... they drove the Varangians behind the sea... and began to control themselves... and they had an intestine strife... And they told to themselves: 'Let us look for a prince who would possess us and judge us according to the law.' And they went abroad, to the Varangian Russes. And the Chud, Slavs, Krivichi and Ves told to the Russes: 'Our land is large and rich, but there is no order in it. Come to rule and reign over us.' They thus selected three brothers, with their kinfolk, who took with them all the Russes and went to the Slavs and the oldest, Rùrik, located himself in Novgorod…" This is how *The Tale of Bygone Years* describes the calling of Rurik to the Slavic lands. We do not know exactly where did this half-legendary Varangian *konung* come from nor what were his deeds on the Novgorod land – it is sufficient that he became the founder of the first Russian ruling dynasty. Before his death in 879 Rurik entrusted the tutorship of his little son Igor to Oleg, either his relation or closest associate.

Unknown Russian engraver.
The genealogical tree *Grand Princes and Tsars of Russia*. 1810–30. SM "Peterhof"

Rurik's Arrival to the Slavonic Lands. From the book *History of the Russian State: 862–1884*. 1885

Princess Olga's Vengeance to the Drevliane for the Death of Prince Igor. From the book *History of the Russian State. 862–1884*. 1885

In 945 Igor, Prince of Kiev, went with his host to the Slavic tribe of the Drevliane and forced them to pay a double tribute and then came back with a small detachment to collect a new tribute. The indignant Drevliane killed Igor and his "small host". On killing Igor the Drevliane decided that they are free from their obligations to the Kiev Dynasty. They demanded Princess Olga to marry the Drevliane's Prince Mala and sent their envoys to her. Olga cruelly dealt with them and then appeared in the Drevliane land and arranged there a feast to commemorate her husband on his burial ground and invited the Drevliane there. Olga ordered her warriors to treat the Drevliane to wine and when they were drunk the warriors killed them with their swords. In the next year, 946,Olga undertook a new campaign against the Drevliane, she captured their town of Iskorosten and again cruelly dealt with its inhabitants – some of them were killed and some others were given to slavery and still others were to pay a "burdensome tribute".

Detail of painting of The Faceted Chamber. The first members of the Rurik dynasty: Grand Prince Rurik, Grand Prince Igor and Sviatoslav, Igor's son

The ROMANOVS
The Emperors of Russia

Abris Art Publishers

St Petersburg • Peterhof

2007

ВЕЛИКІЕ КНЯЗЬЯ И ЦАРИ РОССІЙСКІЕ

Dessine par Ordonateur

1 РЮРИКЪ родился у варягъ въ 830. Княземъ началъ съ 862 до 879. ДИМІТРІЙ Александрович р1236 с 1276 д1293 зъ АНДРЕЙ
2 ОЛЕГЪ р.855 к съ879 д.а.913 ИГОРЬ рюриковичб. р.877 к съ 913 до 945 ОЛГА Александровичр 1256 к с 1281 д1295 зъ ДАНІИ Александровичр1261 к с1303 зъ МИХ
к съ 945 съ 965 ъ СВЯТОСЛАВЪ Игоревичб. р.933 к съ 958 д 973 зъ ЯРОПОЛКЪ АИЛЪ Ярославовичр 1261 к с1319 д1312 зъ ЮРІЙ ш Даниловичб. р 1281 к 1320 д1325 зъ А
Святославовичр. 938. к съ 973 д 980. зъ ВЛАДИМИРЪ Святославовичр 955 к с 981. ЛЕКСАНДРЪ зъ Михайловичр1294 к 1326 д1339 зъ ІОАНЪ Даниловичб р1300 к с1328
д1015 зъ СВЯТОПОЛКЪ Ярославовичр. 983 к 1015. ЯРОСЛАВЪ Владимеровичр. 978 к1016. 28 д 1340. зъ СИМЕОНЪ Іоанновичр1320 с1340 д1353. зъ ІОАНЪ Іоанновичр1326
105 д1054 ИЗЯСЛАВЪ Ярославовичр1019 к съ 1054 д1073 зъ СВЯТОСЛАВЪ Ярославовичр1027 к1073 к 1353 д 1359. ДИМІТРІ

The Moscow Kremlin. Detail of the painting of the Golden Tsarina's Chamber. The recognition of Olga in Tsargrad (Constantinople)

It was that Oleg (described in Pushkin's *Tale about the Prophetic Oleg*) who would unite the Novgorodian and Kievan lands under him in 882 and would declare Kiev the capital – "the mother of all Russian cities", undertake victorious campaigns to Constantinople and hand over the enlarged state to his pupil, Igor, Rurik's son (912–945). Among the first rulers of the Rurik dynasty is the only woman who ruled the ancient Russian state – Princess Olga (945–964), Igor's widow. People called her in different ways: Sly Olga – for her sophisticated and harsh vengeance to the Drevliane guilty of her husband's death; St Olga – for she was the first of the Kievan rulers to convert to Christianity; Wise Olga – for she regulated tax collecting from subjugated tribes, sought to establish peaceful relations with neighbours and was in charge of Kiev while her son, Sviatoslav (964–972), waged numerous wars.

The Baptism of Russia.
From the book *History of the Russian State: 862–1884.* 1885

The process of conversion to Christianity of the entire Kievan Rus was long and difficult – it lasted for more than a century and some Slavic tribes finally adopted the new Orthodox Christian faith only by the 13th century.

However, it was not Olga who baptized the entire Old Rus – this merit belonged to her grandson Vladimir the Red Son (980–1015). The historian Sergei Solovyev wrote about him: "... Vladimir had a broad soul... that made him the red sun for the people... Vladimir liked to think with his host and liked to feast with it, and legend have remained about his feasts in chronicles and in songs." Kievan Rus attained true flowering under Yaroslav, Vladimir's son (1019–1054). For his clever state activity and concern for people's education he became known as Yaroslav "the Wise". Many European ruling houses were related to the Grand Prince of Kiev – his daughters became consorts of the Kings of France, Hungary and Norway and his sons married the Polish, German and even Byzantine Princesses.

With the death of Yaroslav the Rurik family broke into numerous branches, of which the most significant for Russia became the family of the Princes of Suzdal, the descendants of Prince Yury, the founder of Moscow Yury Dolgoruky or Yury the Long-Armed (1132–1157), son of Vladimir Monomachus. Among the descendants of Prince Yury was such a prominent figure as Prince Alexander Nevsky, who defended the Fatherland and the Orthodox faith from Swedish and German knights in those difficult years.

The Moscow Kremlin. The Archangel
Cathedral. Fresco: *St Prince Alexander
Nevsky*. 1652–1666

The Great Kremlin Palace.
The Alexander Hall. Otto Friedrich
Moller, *The Battle of the Neva*. 1856

Alexander Nevsky (1220–1263) owes his
name to his victory over the Swedes on
the Neva River (1240). He was not only
an army commander, but also a wise
political leader, who not once saved
the Russian state by means of diplomatic
talks from the Tatar Khans' devastating
incursions and requisitions. Even in his
lifetime he enjoyed a great respect of
his subjects and soon after his death
the first hagiographic life of St Alexander
was written that emphasized the true
sanctity of the prince.

*Alexander Nevsky Asking the Khan for
Mercy to the Russian Land*.
From the book *History of the Russian
State: 862–1884*. 1885

The Moscow Kremlin.
The Archangel Cathedral. Fresco:
Grand Duke Ivan Kalita. 1652–66

Ivan Kalita (*ca*. 1280–1340), the younger son of Prince Daniel, became the third Moscow ruler, but often he is regarded as the founder of the Moscow Dynasty. Indeed, it was he who defeated Tver and annexed new territories to Moscow and strengthened its economic position (hence his nickname *Kalita*, meaning "Purse" in Russian). In his reign Moscow became the seat of the Metropolitan of All the Russias and the spiritual centre of the Russian lands.

His grandson, the Moscow Prince Ivan Kalita (1325–1340), ensured to the Russian people by his flexible policy with regard to the Golden Horde 40 years of quiet life without devastating incursions of the Mongols and laid the foundations of the might of the Moscow Principality. It is believed that one of the Prince's associates was Andrei Kobyla, the ancestor of the Zakharyin-Romanov family.

Several decades later the grandson of Ivan Kalita, Prince Dmitry or Demetrius (1359–1389), won a brilliant victory over Khan Mamai on the Kulikovo Field. This victory testified that the idea of the union of the Russia lands for the sake of victory over the enemy and for the flowering of Russia captured the Russians' minds.

But it was only 100 years later, on 12 November 1480, after the two armies met on the Ugra River and the scared Tatars retreated without fighting that the power of the Horde's Khans over Russia was completely overthrown. And it as also in the same period that the formation of the unified Moscow state was completed. The unification of Russia and the defeat of the Horde were achieved under Ivan III, the Grand Duke and Sovereign of all the Russias (1462–1505).

The Moscow Kremlin. The Archangel Cathedral. *St John the Forerunner*. Moscow.
16th century. Icon of Tsar Ivan the Terrible's name saint

Tsar Ivan IV, nicknamed the Terrible (1530–1584)

On 16 January 1547 Grand Prince Ivan IV Vasilyevich adopted the title of the Tsar. The Moscow Principality turned into the Russian State.

The Moscow Kremlin. The Archangel Cathedral. Liturgical cuffs. Donation of Tsarina Marpha Matveyevna. Moscow. Second half of the 17th century

The Moscow Kremlin. The Archangel Cathedral. Altar cross. Moscow. 1560

Tsar Ivan Vasilyevich at the Tomb of His Son. From the book *History of the Russian State: 862–1884.* 1885

The death of his son, Tsarevich Ivan, struck Ivan the Terrible to the heart of hearts. With the death of Ivan a whole dynastic line had been interrupted and now the Tsar's second son, the childless Fiodor, generally thought to be hardly able to rule, came to become the successor.

In the sixteenth century, the seventh century of its rule, the ancient dynasty was apparently at its sunset. This was revealed in the conduct and activities of Ivan IV (1533–1584) known as Ivan the Terrible (suffice it to mention countless victims of the Streltsy's terror). The fate of his sons also confirms this statement. Tsarevich Ivan died from a blow by his father's staff, while his younger son, Demetrius, was mortally ill. The last Tsar of the Rurik Dynasty was Fiodor of Theodore (1584–1598), the middle son of Ivan IV by Anastasia Zakharyina. The Rurik Dynasty of Russia's founders and gatherers would break with his demise.

After the death of the childless Theodore the throne turned to be captured by the Tsar's brother-in-law Boris Godunov. "There will be no rich or poor people in my kingdom," he declared in public during his coronation and taking the collar of his richly embroidered shirt, added: "And I'll share this last shirt with all of you!" However, in the late sixteenth and early seventeenth centuries Russia had to live through the Time of Troubles. The country and its people suffered a lot of trials and tribulations during some twenty years of confusion and disarray: a terrible famine and great mortality, rebellions that spread over huge territories, the first wave of false rulers in the history of Russia and the invasion of the Swedish and Polish armies and, at last, the endless succession of rulers on the Moscow throne.

Tsar Fiodor Ivanovich (1557–1598)

Fiodor Ivanovich or Theodore, the middle son of Ivan the Terrible, became the Tsar of Russia at the age of 27. Many of his contemporaries, especially foreign ones, thought him to be 'simple in mind" or, to say it bluntly, he was weak-minded. Common people, however, liked his piousness and kind heart. It was even said that only thanks to Theodore's constant praying Russia managed to improve its economic situation by the end of the sixteenth century. However, an indubitable fact is Theodore's subjugation to his beloved wife, Irina Godunova, and her brother Boris.

The Moscow Kremlin.
The Archangel Cathedral.
Phelonion. Donation of Tsar Boris Godunov in 1602. Moscow.
Late 16th century

Tsar Boris Godunov (1552–1605)

The reign of Boris Godunov began even during the life of Tsar Theodore, although he was crowned for the Russian throne in September 1898. The former *oprichnik*, a clever and cunning politician and an experienced schemer, he seemed to be too dangerous to the Moscow boyars – many rumours were spread about Godunov's engagement in the mysterious deaths, such as the tragic death of Tsarevich Demetrius.

Despite Godunov's certain achievements: the establishment of the Patriarchate in Russia, the construction of a number of cities on the Volga and the erection of new magnificent structures in Moscow, the victorious war with Sweden and sending a group of young members of the gentry abroad to study – he failed to get a strong position on the throne and to become the founder of a new royal dynasty. At the end of May 1605, just a month and a half after the death of Boris and the proclamation of his son Theodore as Tsar, the Muscovites opened the city gate to the army led by the man who declared himself to be the miraculously saved Tsarevich Demetrius, the legal heir to the Russian throne, but who was Grigory Otrepyev in reality. The sixteen-year-old Theodore was killed and False Demetrius I ruled Moscow for a year.

Tsar Demetrius (Grigory Otrepyev, 1577–1606)

In 1604 a tailed comet appeared in the sky over Russia – a harbinger of disaster, in the notions of seventeenth-century people. In the same year the "miraculously saved Tsarevich Demetrius of Uglich" appeared in the Rzeczpospolita. That was a young adventurer Grigory Otrepyev, a former serf of the boyar Romanov family, who ran away to Poland from the Chudov Monastery. With the aid of Polish magnates and the section of Russian society displeased with Boris Godunov he managed to take the Moscow throne for a year.

The Moscow Kremlin. The Archangel Cathedral. Cap of Tsarevich Demetrius. 1580s

In the course of a new rebellion in the capital provoked by Otrepyev's desire to rule ignoring the boyars and by his marriage to the proud Polish lady Marina Mniszech the Pretender was killed and Prince Vasily Shiusky was proclaimed the new Tsar.

His five-year reign, however, did not make the people's life easier. At first the revolt of Ivan Bolotnikov, who claimed to be "the voivode Demetrius" and managed to come close to Moscow, broke out. Hardly completing the destruction of Bolotnikov's forces, they learned about the emergence of "Tsarevich Demetrius" – the second impostor – at Russia's western borders. He also failed to capture Moscow and had to establish his headquarters in the village of Tushino near Moscow. This led to the emergence of the second centre of power, in parallel to Moscow, with the Tsar, army, Duma and even the Patriarch Philaretes (Fiodor Nikitich Romanov in secular life, and many Russian districts swore allegiance to the "Tushino Thief" as the Pretender was later known. Shuisky failed to keep power in his hands even on obtaining a detachment of Swedish troops invited by him (this made the Rzeczpospolita begin their undisguised invasion) and was deposed in July 1610. The Boyar government, the Semiboyarshchina, concluded a treaty with Poland to let the King's son Wladyslaw, become the Russian Tsar. Moscow turned out to be in the hands of the Poles.

The Martyr Tsarevich Demetrius of Uglich

Patriarch Philaretes (ca 1550–1633)

Patriarch Philaretes or Fiodor Nikitich Romanov in secular life, a famous Moscow dandy, was a strong rival of Boris Godunov striving to get power. For this reason he fell in disgrace and was forced to become a monk with the name of Philaretes. Philaretes played an important role during the Time of Trouble. On returning in 1619 from the Polish captivity, Philaretes was elevated to the Patriarchate. Until his death he was the actual co-ruler of his son and officially had the title of the "Great Sovereign".

Tsar Michael or Mikhail Fiodorovich Romanov (1596–1645).

He was distinguished by meekness, mercy and piety. Tsar Michael established in the country the church feast in honour of the icon of Our Lady of Kazan – the heavenly patron of the Romanov family.

We can only guess how the events would develop in Russia, but the firm position of Patriarch Hermogen, who even from his imprisonment appealed to the Russians to fight the invaders. The appeals found a response in the plans of the First Zemstvo Militia and in the glorious victories of the Second Militia led by Prince Dmitry Pozharsky and the city headman Kozma Minin.

In October 1612 the national army of Minin and Pozharsky liberated Moscow from the Poles. On 21 February 1613 the Zemstvo Council elected the sixteen-year-old Mikhail Romanov to rule Russia as Tsar Michael, the Sovereign of All the Russias. Since Michael's grandfather, the boyar Nikita, was a brother of Ivan IV's wife, Anastasia, the Romanovs could claim for the throne already after the death of Theodore. But it was Boris Godunov who was elected the Tsar and in order to get rid of this dangerous rival, made Fiodor take monastic vows with the name of Philaretes.

Tsar Michael had to solve difficult problems in order to promote further revival of the country. With this aim in view the state machinery and the local system of control were strengthened. Towards the 1640s the economical crisis had been overcome. Mining came to be developed, the first manufactories and works appeared and expansion to Siberia continued.

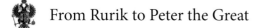

Procession to the Assumption
Cathedral on the day of
the Coronation of Mikhail
Romanov

In February 1613, when
the Zemstvo Assembly was
electing a new tsar for Russia,
Mikhail Romanov was not even
present in Moscow. Together
with his mother, Nun Martha,
he was in the Hepatius
Monastery near Kostroma
and knew nothing about
a new turn in his destiny.
The crowning of the first
Tsar in the Romanov Dynasty
with the cap of Monomachus
was held on 11 July 1613 in
the Assumption Cathedral in
the Moscow Kremlin.

Unknown
engraver.
*Tsar Michael
Giving
Audience
to Foreign
Ambassadors.*
1647.
SM
"Peterhof"

Tsar Alexis or Alexei Mikhailovich (1629–1676)

He knew well foreign languages and theology,
liked spiritual music and was the first of
the Russian Tsars who began to edit and sign
decrees by his own hand. The Tsar was placid,
communicative, inquisitive and hilarious. His
favourite pastime was falconry, and he even
wrote a special work devoted to this subject.

The first Tsar of the Romanov
Dynasty was married twice. His first
wife, Maria Dolgorukaya, died in a
year after their wedding. He had ten
children by his second wife, Yevdokia
Streshneva. Tsar Michael died on 13
July 1645, at 49 years sharp.

His 16-year-old son, Alexei
Mikhailovich, or Alexis, succeeded
him on the throne. Tsar Alexis is
known in Russian history as the "Qui-

Olearius. *The Tsar's and Patriarch's Grand Entrée from the Kremlin.*

In the 1650s the Tsar befriended with Nikon, the future Patriarch, the ideologist of the well-known reform of the Russian Orthodox Church that led to Schism. Nikon succeeded in introducing Byzantine orders in church rituals and correcting the church books according to the Greek examples, but he failed to repeat the career of Patriarch Philaretes by becoming the co-ruler of Alexis. In 1666 the Holy Assembly deposed Nikon and deprived him of the Patriarch's rank.

etest" Sovereign, although the years of his reign can hardly be called quiet. The Salt (1648), Bread (1650) and Copper Coin (1662) Riots, the Solovetsky uprising (1668–1676) and the revolt of Stepan Razin (1670–1671) occurred in his reign. The reign of Alexis is remarkable for other event, too. In 1649 a new legal code, the *Sobornoye Ulozheniye* or *The Code* was introduced, which legalized serfdom among other things. Regiments modelled on foreign units were formed in the army and an attempt was made to build ships for the defence of trade caravans on the Caspian Sea. The autocratic power strengthened in the country.

Tsar Alexis followed in the footsteps of his father, trying to settle principal problems of foreign policy. One of the most important achievements was the union of the Ukraine with Russia in 1654. The complete exploration of Siberia was promoted by the expeditions of Semion Dezhnev, Vasily Poyarkov and Yerofei Khabarov. Attempts to fight back an outlet to the Baltic Sea were not so successful – the war against Sweden ended in a disastrous failure.

Alexei Mikhailovich married twice. In 1647 his wedding with Maria Miloslavskaya took place. After her death he married Natalia Naryshkina and she gave birth to Tsarevich Piotr and two daughters. Tsar Alexis died in the night of 30 January 1676 and left the throne to his elder son, Fiodor or Theodore. Alexis was buried, like his father, Tsar Michael, in the Cathedral of the Archangel Michael in the Moscow Kremlin.

PETER I

Piotr Alexeyevich, called "the Great"
(30 May 1672, Moscow – 28 January, 1725, St Petersburg)
the Tsar of Russia from 27 April 1682,
the Emperor from 22 October 1721

Peter was born in the marriage of the Russian Tsar Alexei Mikhailovich and the Tsarina Natalia Kirillovna Naryshkina. She was the Tsar's second wife. He married Natalia Naryshkina, an ordinary nobleman's daughter, on 22 January 1671. Alexei Mikhailovich had thirteen children by his first marriage to Maria Miloslavskaya, who died in 1669. After the death of Tsar Alexei Mikhailovich his elder son, Fiodor or Theodore, a weak and sickly man, came to the throne and ruled Russia for a short period until his demise in the spring of 1682. After that, on 27 April 1682, the boyars pushed to the throne the youngest son of Alexei Mikhailovich, Tsarevich Peter, a clever and agile ten-year-old boy, instead of his half-brother, the sixteen-year-old Tsarevich Ivan, the next in the line, who was sick and feeble-minded. Thus the so-called "Naryshkin party" got the upper hand at the court. Dissatisfied with the situation, the group headed by the Miloslavsky family made a coup and provoked a revolt of common people and the Streltsy. In May 1682 the rebels burst into the Kremlin, murdered all the nearest relatives of Tsarina Natalia and declared Tsarevich Ivan, or Ivan V, Peter's co-ruler. Soon, on 29 May 1682, Tsarevna Sophia, the half-sister of the juvenile Tsars, became the Regent. It was she who aspired to supreme power and eventually seized it.

Unknown Russian artist.
Portrait of Emperor Peter the Great. Early 18th century. SM "Peterhof"

Tsar Alexis (1629–1676),
father of Peter the Great.

Tsarina Natalia Naryshkina (1651–1694),
the second wife of Tsar Alexis,
mother of Peter the Great.

V. Schwarz. *The Tsarina's Spring Pilgrimage Train in the Reign of Tsar Alexis Mikhailovich*. 1868

Tsar Theodore or Fiodor Alexeyevich (1661–1682), son of Tsar Alexis and his first wife, Maria Miloslavskaya. Tsar Theodore was well educated, pious and had a bent for literary occupation; his tutor was the Enlightener and poet Simeon Polotsky, who made his pupil a knowledgeable man.

Tsar Peter I, called the Great (1672–1725).

Son of Tsar Alexis and Natalia Naryshkina. He began to rule as the Tsar in 1682 and as the first Emperor of Russia in 1721.

Tsar Ivan V or Ioann Alexeyevich (1666–1696), son of Tsar Alexis and Maria Miloslavskaya, Peter the Great's step-brother. In 1682 he was proclaimed Tsar together with Peter. Badly ill, Ivan did not participate in state affairs and after the capture of power by the Naryshkin group in 1689 he was completely removed from governing.

The bloody scenes of the Naryshkins' massacre by the Streltsy imprinted on Peter's memory forever. The fear did not leave Peter later, too, when the boy, his mother and their nearest associates sheltered from troubles in the suburban palace at Preobrazhenskoye. So Peter then hated forever the Streltsy, old Moscow, and all things "ancient" and fiercely fought against them. He grew at Preobrazhenskoye as a lively, inquisitive boy and early revealed an interest in everything associated with the army and devoted all his time to military games and "toy" battles. He had no wise tutors and did not receive the thorough education due to a successor – he studied with intervals and not very diligently, as the predominant features of his character were unrestrained impulsiveness and self-will.

Tsarevna Sophia (1657–1704), daughter of Tsar Alexis Mikhailovich and Maria Miloslavskaya, the half-sister of Peter the Great. Regent from 1682 under the Co-Tsars Ivan and Peter.

Co-Tsars Ivan and Peter.
Engraving from the *Coronation
Album*. 1689. This double
official portrait of the brothers
from the time when they
ruled together (1682–96)
was to convince society
that political situation was
stable. In real fact, however,
behind the curtains of this
idyllic scene passions were
boiling and a struggle of court
groupings was under way.

S. Zubov from a drawing by I. Zarudny. *The Boat of Peter the Great*. 1722

In August 1689 the "Naryshkin Party" succeeded in overthrowing Sophia and her clan. Tsar Ivan V, unable to fulfil his royal duties, was finally pushed into the background. Peter, however, did not take pains to get control of the state into his hands because he was engrossed with his favourite pastimes – the building of ships and military maneuvres.

I. Repin. *Tsarevna Sophia in a Year after Her Confinement to the New Maiden Convent, during the Execution of the Streltsy and the Tortures of All Her Servants in 1698*. 1879. The Tretyakov Gallery

The clever, resolute and well-educated Sophia dreamed of getting rid of Tsar Peter and becoming the Sovereign. However, during the years of her regency she failed to strengthen her authority so that society would follow her and therefore she was defeated. Her closest adherents were executed or exiled and Sophia herself was confined to the New Maiden Convent, where in 1698, after the suppression of the revolt of the Streltsy, she was forced to take the veil. She died in the convent in 1704.

V. Surikov. *The Morning of the Execution of the Streltsy*. 1881. The Tretyakov Gallery

He fully matured in the course of two campaigns against the Turkish fortress of Azov carried out in 1695 and 1696. Since then Peter considered himself to be "in the service" to the state and this formula precisely characterizes his attitude to his duty. Having no idea as to how to transform the "old ways", he undertook a trip to Europe. Disguised as a rank-and-file volunteer nobleman of the Great Embassy (1697–98), he visited Prussia, Holland and England, where he trained as a shipwright and artillery man and acquainted himself with the customs and morals of foreign peoples.

A. Schoonebeck. *The Siege of Azov in 1696*. 1699–1700

The capture of the Azov Fortress became the young Tsar's first success. Later Peter stated that under the walls of Azov he began his service to the Fatherland.

Unknown engraver.
Peter the Great Meeting Louis XV, King of France, in Paris. First half of the 18th century

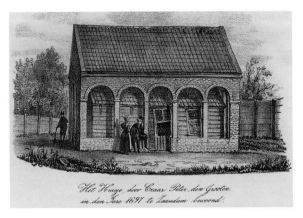

Unknown engraver. *The house of Peter the Great at Saardam in 1697.*
SM "Peterhof"

Peter liked Holland from his youth – the Dutchmen living in
the German Settlement in Moscow trained him in various crafts
and he learned the Dutch language from them. He trained as a
shipwright and took a course of ship-building at the shipyard
in the Dutch town of Saardam (now Saandam). Peter rented a
small house and lived there for several days, but then he left for
Amsterdam, to train at the shipyard of the East India Company,
because crowds of curious idlers used to come to see the unusual
Russian Tsar and he could not even walk by Saardam streets.

Ye. Grigoryev. *Peter the Great at the Shipyard
in Saardam*. 1872

L. Bernstamm.
*Peter the Great
as a Saardam
Shipwright*. 1910.
SM "Peterhof"

Peter's associate, Franz
Lefort (1656–1699).

A participant in military
campaigns, General-Admiral
Lefort was known for his
light and merry temper,
he could talk several
languages and fulfilled a
lot of diplomatic missions.
It was not without his hint
that Peter conceived to
send the Great Embassy
to the European courts.
The Tsar liked Lefort very
much and was very grievous
after his sudden death.

Alexander Menshikov (1673–1729)

Peter the Great was encircled with his adherents and associates who were later called the "fledglings of Peter's nest". The most notable among them was Alexander Menshikov. His name is mentioned for the first time in 1698. Foreigners characterized him in a disparaging way as "the Tsar's favourite Alexashka of humble origin". He began from the position of the Tsar's orderly and attained the highest ranks in the state. Menshikov was a truly talented man. He distinguished himself for the first time during the storming of the Nöteburg (Oreshek) Fortress in the autumn of 1702 – it was his bold action that proved to be decisive in the battle for the fortress. Later he was appointed the Commandant of this fortress (renamed Schlüsselburg) and this time excelled as an administrator. With the foundation of St Petersburg Menshikov was appointed its Governor General and also supervised the construction of the new capital. Menshikov distinguished himself in the battles of the Northern War as the president of the Military Collegium (or Ministry); he was a cavalier of many awards, had the title of the Most Illustrious Prince and in 1727 became a Generalissimo. But he was at the same time he was a money-grubber and embezzler of public funds, so finally he accumulated immense reaches. Many times the prince was often caught, but he was lucky to escape the scaffold and whip thanks to Peter and his own ability to repent and to freely return the stolen money to the state.

Jacob Bruce (1670–1735)

A descendant of the Scottish Kings, Jacob Bruce was one of the most authoritative men of his time. An eminent scholar, a specialist in engineering, he was in charge of the reform of Russian artillery, organization of artillery production and gained outstanding success in this field – Russian artillery became one of the best in Europe. He also fulfilled Peter's diplomatic missions. But Bruce was especially fond of science; he devoted all his spare time to experiments.

Andrei Ostermann (1686–1747)

Andrei Ostermann, son of a pastor from the German town of Bohum, a student of the Jena University, killed his friend in a quarrel and fled first to Holland and then to Russia. He became an interpreter, attracted Peter's attention and the Tsar took him to the diplomatic service. Towards the end of Peter's reign Ostermann made an outstanding career and became a Count, Russia's Vice-Chancellor.

The Battle off Gangut in 1714

A. Sparre. *Portrait of Charles XII.* 1712

Charles XII, the King of mighty Sweden, was Peter's main enemy in the Northern War. Peter revealed himself as a talented army commander in the crucial Battle of Poltava. Boris Sheremetev was at the head of the Russian infantry, Alexander Menshikov commanded the cavalry and Jacob Bruce supervised artillery. The Swedes ran away from the battlefield. Sweden was defeated and a new strong state appeared in the East that gained important sea ports on the Baltic Sea. Peter, however, eagerly wanted to advance Russia to the European political stage and continued the war until a brilliant complete victory.

L. Caravaque. *The Battle of Poltava.* 1717–18

On his return to Russia, the Tsar began his radical reforms that would change the country within two decades. He made great changes in the system of governing, finance and trade, created a new army, built the fleet and industry. The changes touched literally all aspects of Russian people's life from their public service to outward appearance. Having conquered Ingria or Ingermanland during the Northern War of 1700–21, Peter founded St Petersburg in 1703 to turn it into the capital of Russia in 1712. Here, in his favourite "paradise", after the victorious end of the war on 22 October 1721, he was proclaimed the Emperor of Russia and thus the Russian Empire began to exist.

Sundial. England. Craftsman: J. Rowley. 1715. SM "Peterhof"

The sundial was commissioned by George I of England as a diplomatic gift to Peter the Great and handed over to him through S.G. Naryshkin, the Russian ambassador, in 1715.

Suit of Peter the Great.
The Berlin Workshops. 1720s.
SM "Peterhof"

PETRUS I. sive MAGNUS
RUSSORUM OMNIUM IMPERATOR & AUTOCRATOR
Quid in Cælo rerum. Pelagoque geratur
Et Tellure videt: totumq inquirit in Orbem. Ovid.

B. Vogel from the original by I. Kupetzky. *Emperor Peter the Great.* 1737. SM "Peterhof"

Peter's unusual height, simple manners, negligence in dress, emphatically modest way of living, rare capacity for hard work exemplary for his subjects, insatiable intellectual curiosity and vigour struck his contemporaries. The range of his interests was unusually wide. He always respected only exact and natural sciences and did not recognize anything abstract, having no practical value. The Tsar liked to contact with sailors, smiths and machine inventors; he could explore the collections of foreign rarities for hours and assiduously earned various crafts. But his favourite occupation was shipbuilding and sailing in order to check now and again his knowledge and skills as a shipwright and sailor.

Gavrila Golovkin
(1660–1734)

The Head of the Ambassadorial Chancellery, Senator, President of the Collegium of Foreign Affairs. In 1706 he became the first Chancellor of Russia. Being not a man of brilliant gifts, Golovkin was reliable, cautious, efficient and dependable, and he had no enemies. Thanks to that he remained in his very responsible position until his death comfortably, respected by everybody.

Boris Sheremetev
(1652–1719)

Field Marshal, participant of Peter's campaigns. He came from a boyar family and was a professional soldier; he participated in all Russia's wars since the 1680s. His distinctive quality was reliability. He was one of the first Russian to adopt European customs and clothes.

Fiodor Apraxin
(1661–1728)

Admiral, President of the Admiralty Collegium. Brother of Tsar Theodore's wife Marpha Matveyevna, Apraxin was near Peter the Great from the very first years of his reign. As "a faithful servant of the Fatherland", as a disciplinary, conscientious and honest man, Apraxin commanded the Russian Fleet for a quarter of a century, although in fact Peter the Great himself was at the head of the naval forces.

Piotr Shafirov
(1669–1739)

Diplomat, Vice-Chancellor and Vice-President of the Collegium of Foreign Affairs. He began his career as an interpreter of the Ambassadorial Prikaz. Thanks to his refined mind, flexibility and capacity for court intrigues Shafirov became one of Peter's closest associates, a keen diplomat, who saved the Russian Army from capitulation on the Pruth River in 1711. In 1723, however, he fell in disgrace and was even sentenced to death, but then pardoned and exiled to the North.

It was difficult for people to live near the Tsar. A restless and unpredictable man, with abrupt changes in his mood from gaiety to fury, Peter was sometimes suspicious and mistrustful. His famous cudgel used to fall, frequently with no reason at all, on the backs of his dignitaries or servants, who happened to appear nearby in the heat of the moment. Peter's crude manners, repulsive habits and insults to his entourage struck foreigners. The convulsive twitching of his face and hands – the undoubted symptom of a fit of unrestrained rage – scared people around him. But all the unfavourable impressions of this tall jerking man in worn-down shoes became insignificant under the influence of the amazement and delight aroused by Peter's profound mind, his subtle, imaginative and faithful judgements, his true wisdom as a politician. Usually unbridled and hot-tempered, the Tsar turned into a patient and composed diplomat at the negotiating table. Thanks to his energetic foreign policy Peter succeeded in enlarging the limits of his Empire, laying down the foundations for its prosperity, and became an outstanding figure in world history.

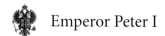

The construction of St Petersburg was Peter's primary concern. He loved his young city from the very beginning and called it "Paradise". Here, at a distance from hated Moscow, he founded his capital. The basis of St Petersburg was a fortress on Hare Island that was originally called "Sankt-Pieterburgh". It was only later that the name of the fortress passed to the city itself and the citadel came to be named the Peter and Paul Fortress. Erected to a design of German and French architects, with additions by Peter himself, the fortress served as an insuperable obstacle for the Swedes. Opposite the fortress Peter had two palaces built for him – the Summer and the Winter Palaces. The first of them has reached us unaltered, whereas the latter was reconstructed many times and over the years completely lost its original shape of a cosy two-storey building in the Dutch style.

A. Rostovtsev. *The Gostiny Dvor Trading Arcade.* 1716

Right near the Peter and Paul Fortress, on the City Side (later renamed the St Petersburg Side) the building of state establishments and dwelling houses began to grow. In the centre of the square stood the Church of the Holy Trinity, where Peter used to pray. Next to it there was a pier and foreign ships moored to it. Stretching along the other side of the square was the vast Gostiny Dvor Trading Arcade.

Unknown engraver. *The First Winter Palace of Peter the Great.* 1716–17. On the bank of the Neva stood the two-storey Winter Palace with an attic built in 1711–17.

P. Novelli. *Peter the Great at the Construction of St Petersburg.* Second half of the 18th century

A. Zubov (?).
The Admiralty. 1716

In 1705 they began to build ships in St Petersburg. Drawing on the example of England and Holland, on the left bank of the Neva was erected the Admiralty that combined a shipyard, warehouses and office for fleet management. The Admiralty was crowned by a tall tower with a clock and the spire soaring to the sky of St Petersburg was surmounted with a small ship, a symbol of the city.

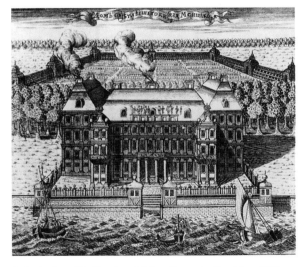

A. Rostovtsev. *The Mansion of Prince Alexander Menshikov*. 1716

The palace or residence of the first Governor General of St Petersburg was put up between 1710 and 1727. But a house-warming party was held there as early as 1 October 1711 and in 1712 it was the venue of the weddings of Boris Sheremetev and Yakov Dolgoruky.

"The mansion of Prince Menshikov is the earliest and most magnificent on Vasilyevsky Island... Built in brick, in the Italian style, it has three stories... There are lots of apartments in the house and all are richly furnished". From the book *The Description of St Petersburg*, 1716–17

The Tsar was unhappy in his private life. His first marriage to Yevdokia Lopukhina, the *okolnichy's* daughter, contracted at the behest of his mother on 27 May 1689, proved to be unfortunate. Of their three children only the elder son Alexei survived, but he grew up in the atmosphere of hate to his father, who divorced Tsarina Yevdokia in 1698 and confined her in a convent at Suzdal, where she was forced to take monastic vows with the name of Helen. Tsarevich Alexei was antagonistic to his father's values. And although the son did not claim for power, his status as the heir to the throne caused the Tsar to be afraid for Russia's future.

Tsarevich Alexei (1690–1718), son of Peter the Great and his first wife Yevdokia Lopukhina

From his early years the Tsarevich grew up without his mother who was confined in a convent. He felt alien to his father too, as Peter had another family. A stubborn and strong-willed like his father, he did not like Peter and denounced the reforms started by him. The people around Alexei supported him in his opposition to his father.

Crown-Princess Charlotte Christine Sophie of Braunschweig-Wolfenbüttel (1694–1715), wife of Tsarevich Alexei

Married against her will, she did not like her husband and lingered with her arrival in Russia and when she came to St Petersburg, she could not get accustomed to living here: she remained a Lutheran, did not know the Russian language and suffered from solitude. Her husband was quite cool to her. She died after the birth of her son, Piotr, but rumour was spread that the Crown Princess ran away leaving the body of her servant who had died a day before instead of herself, but that was not true.

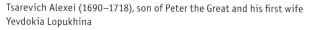

L. Caravaque. *Portrait of Tsarevich Piotr Alexeyevich and Tsarevna Natalia Alexeyevna As Apollon and Diane*. 1722. The Tretyakov Gallery

From 1727 Piotr Alexeyevich reigned under the name of Peter II.

The fear increased when Charlotte, the Tsarevich's wife, gave birth to two children, a daughter, Natalia, in 1714 and a son, Piotr, in 1715. Notably, the Tsar's second wife, Yekaterina Alexeyevna (known later as Catherine I), gave birth to a son, also called Piotr, almost simultaneously with Charlotte. This led to a conflict between Peter the Great and Tsarevich Alexei that was largely provoked by the Tsar himself. In 1716, afraid for his life, the Tsesarevich used the opportunity to escape to Austria, but was discovered there by Russian agents. Alexei was enticed to Russia by deceit – Peter's emissary gave him a letter with his father's solemn promise not to persecute the son. After he had renounced his rights for the throne in public, however, the Tsarevich was arrested in March 1718 and tortured (in the presence of the Tsar himself). On 24 June 1718 the special court condemned Alexei to death for treason by orders of Peter the Great and in two days he was secretly killed (strangled or poisoned) in the Peter and Paul Fortress.

N. Gay. *Peter the Great Interrogating Tsarevich Alexei at Peterhof*. 1871

The confrontation of Peter and his son was bitter. Peter did not trust Alexei's ostentatious obedience, interrogated his son about his accomplices and intentions himself and was even present at Alexei's tortures in the torture-chamber. After the pronouncement of death sentence to the Tsarevich Peter ordered to carry it out.

L. Caravaque. *Portrait of Tsarevich Piotr Petrovich As Cupid.*
The Tretyakov Gallery

Tsarevich Piotr Petrovich (1715–1719), son of Peter the
Great and Catherine. After the abdication of Alexei Petrovich he was proclaimed heir to the throne, but soon died.

The removal of Alexei as the successor
was playing into the hands of the Tsarina,
Peter's beloved wife Catherine. A peasant
woman then named Martha Skavronska,
she was taken captive during the seizure
of the Marienburg fortress in Livland by
the Russian army in August 1702. She
passed to the Tsar in 1703 from Alexander Menshikov, whose concubine she had
been before. Martha adopted the Orthodox faith with the name of Yekaterina
Alexeyevna (Tsarevich Alexei was her
godfather) and succeeded in winning the
heart of Peter the Great who got in love
with her and chose her among his other
favourites. On 19 February 1712 the official wedding of Peter and Catherine took
place, although she had been declared
the Tsarina earlier, in 1711. Catherine
gave Peter the Great ten children starting
from 1704, but all of them, except for two
daughters, Anna and Elizabeth, died in

Unknown Russian engraver. *Peter the Great Taking Catherine from Prince Menshikov.* 18th century. SM "Peterhof"

The Tsarevnas Anna Petrovna (1708–1728) and Yelizaveta Petrovna (1709–1761), the daughters of Peter the Great. Peter was fond of them. He never forgot about them in his travels, always sent presents and letters for them and was happy when the girls answered him. They were very different: the dark-haired Anna was reasonable, quiet and shy, the blonde Yelizaveta was derisive, lively and merry. The sisters were friendly and never parted.

L. Caravaque. *Portrait of the Tsarevnas Anna Petrovna and Yelizaveta Petrovna.* 1717. The Russian Museum

infancy. In April 1719 their four-year-old son Piotr, the Tsar's favourite scion, died. The aging Peter the Great had placed great hopes on this son, and it was for the sake of his succession that the Tsar eliminated so cruelly his elder son Alexei. After Piotr's death the Tsar associated all his hopes with Catherine, his "beloved friend".

On 23 December 1721 he declared her the Empress and on 7 May 1724 crowned Catherine in Moscow. It was then perhaps that he signed his will in her favour. However, in the autumn of 1724 Catherine's infidelity with the Chamberlain William Mons was disclosed. The infuriated Peter tore his will declaring Catherine as his successor. Formally accused of bribery, Mons was executed on 6 November and on 22 November Peter signed a contract about the marriage of his daughter Anna to Karl Friedrich, the Duke of Holstein. This hasty decision can be explained by a desire of Peter the Great to pass the throne to Anna's future son, his grandson. According to the marriage contract once a boy were born in this marriage he was to be taken to Peter's court. However, Peter the Great did not live to the day when Anna gave birth to his grandson – the future Emperor Peter III. The founder of the dynasty died in the Winter Palace on 28 January 1725 suffering from terrible physical torments and disquiet about the future of Russia. All the tales about his allegedly said words "Give everything to…" are mere fantasies. To the very end the fifty-two-year-old Emperor hoped to recover and settle all dynastic problems himself. But death prevented him from doing so…

CATHERINE I

Yekaterina Alexeyevna
(5 April 1684, Livland – 6 May 1727, St Petersburg)
the Tsarina from 6 March 1711,
the Empress Consort from 7 May 1724,
the Autocratic Empress from 28 January 1725

The fabulous history of the simple Livland peasant Martha, a common laundress who occupied the Russian throne, is reminiscent of the fairy-tale about Cinderella. Having found herself in Peter's entourage, she captured his heart by her kindness, gaiety and domestic care, by her modest and submissive character. After the death of Peter the Great Alexander Menshikov, Piotr Tolstoy, Pavel Yaguzhinsky and Feofan Prokopovich elevated her to the throne. All of them, Peter's closest associates, were afraid that his grandson (the son of Tsarevich Alexei in whose execution they had participated), the ten-year-old Grand Duke Piotr Alexeyevich, would come to power together with his "old Muscovite" entourage. With the assistance of the guard regiments, who encircled the Winter Palace, the conspirators forced the dignitaries assembled in the palace to approve the election of Catherine I. The new Empress had neither capacity nor desire for the affairs of the state. The burden of state affairs was on Menshikov and the Supreme Secret Council organized in 1726 "at the Empress's side" (as it was written in the decree). In the spring of 1727 she became seriously ill and died.

H. Buchholz. *Portrait of Empress Catherine I.*
The last third of the 18th century.
SM "Peterhof"

Unknown French engraver. *Peter the Great and Catherine I*. 1717.
SM "Peterhof"

I. Zubov. *The Crowning of Empress Yekaterina Alexeyevna
(Catherine I)*. Late 1720s. SM "Peterhof"

Alexander Menshikov (1673–1729)

Menshikov's power peaked under Catherine I.
His main aim now was to become related with
the dynasty by giving his daughter in marriage
for the heir to the throne Piotr Alexeyevich.

Pavel Yaguzhinsky (1683–1736)

Count, diplomat and Procurer-General of the
Senate. His distinctive qualities were honesty
and straightforwardness, for which Peter
especially valued him, calling him his "eye" in
the Senate.

Piotr Tolstoy (1645–1729)

Count, the Chief of Secret Police. A sly and
clever man, he fulfilled many secret missions.
Count Tolstoy tried to struggle against
Menshikov's influence upon Catherine, was
arrested and exiled. He ended his life in
the tower of the Solovetsky Monastery.

A. Zubov. *The Marriage of Peter the Great*. 1712. SM "Peterhof"

The wedding of Peter and Catherine was different from traditional wedding ceremonies of the Russian Tsars. It was modest and Peter invited to it his friends with their wives and sailors. The festivity took place in the Winter Palace under a beautiful chandelier that had been turned on a lathe by the Tsar himself.

Unknown Venetian artist. *View of the Winter Palace of Peter the Great*. 1750s – early 1760s

PETER II

Piotr Alexeyevich
(12 October 1715, St Petersburg – 19 January 1730, Moscow),
the Emperor from 6 May 1727

Born into the family of Tsarevich Alexei and Charlotte, Peter at once lost his mother who died from post-natal fever. Moreover, in 1718 his father was executed by orders of Peter the Great. Grand Duke Piotr Alexeyevich was grown up, together with his elder sister Natalia, at the court of Peter the Great, but the Tsar did not pay much attention to them for he wanted to see on the throne the children of his beloved Catherine. When Peter the Great died on 28 January 1725, many of the dignitaries regarded the grand duke as the real successor. Even in the brief reign of Catherine I the very existence of Peter the Great's grandson exerted a very strong influence on political matters. Alexander Menshikov, the factual ruler of Russia, was particularly inclined to take him into account. On the eve of Catherine's death in the spring of 1727 he managed to get from the Empress the Testament in favour of Grand Duke Piotr, but under the condition that the young Emperor must marry Maria, the daughter of the "Most Illustrious Prince". After the twelve-year-old Peter II had ascended the throne, the real power appeared to be in the hands of Menshikov, who was then promoted to the rank of Generalissimo. He took the young Emperor to his mansion, arranged his engagement to Maria and in general kept the Tsar under persistent and indefatigable control.

J.P. Ludden. *Portrait of Emperor Peter II*. 1728.
The Russian Museum

Maria (1711–1729), daughter of the Most Illustrious Prince Alexander Menshikov, from 1727 the bride of Emperor Peter II, in 1728 exiled together with her father to Beriozovo, where she died.

Ivan Dolgoruky (1708–1739).

In 1726 he was promoted to the rank of Hof-Junker to Grand Duke Piotr Alexeyevich, after Menshikov's fall he was made the Chief Chamberlain, but after the succession of Anna Ioannovna exiled to Beriozov.

However, in the summer of 1727 Menshikov became seriously ill and the young Tsar, oppressed by his surveillance, broke loose from his grip. Menshikov's enemies took an opportunity to their favour and at the beginning of September 1727 the prince was exiled to Siberia. The Tsar, in the company of his flippant friend, the reveller Prince Ivan Dolgoruky, immoderately indulged himself in amusements and pleasures, and the boy was strong enough for that – contemporaries stated his unusually rapid physical development. Under Dolgoruky's influence Peter II developed an interest in hunting. In the early 1728 the court moved to Moscow and the Tsar began to spend time hunting for months in the woods near Moscow. The compiled plan of the young Emperor's education was neglected and he took little interest in state affairs.

The youth produced a painful impression on people around him – he grew up proud and capricious, unkind and secretive. He had a derisive and peevish character and obeyed only to his elder sister Grand Duchess Natalia Alexeyevna, a kind and judicious girl. But in November 1728 she died from galloping consumption. All affairs turned out to be in the hands of Ivan Dolgoruky's relations, with the favourite's father, Prince Alexei Dolgoruky, being particularly influential. By that time St Petersburg had been forgotten and Russia was loosing its political gains as a great power. In 1729 Prince Alexei Dolgoruky conceived to marry Peter II who matured beyond his age to his daughter Princess Yekaterina.

Ch. A. Wortmann. *Portrait of Emperor Peter II*. 1729. SM "Peterhof"

Emperor Peter II

I. Zubov. *Emperor Peter II Going Out in the Village of Izmailovo near Moscow*. Late 1720s

V. Serov. *Emperor Peter II and Tsesarevna Yelizaveta Petrovna Riding to Hounds*. 1900

For some time the Dolgorukys were scared by the burgeoning romance between Peter II and Yelizaveta Petrovna: they often spent time together and used to go hunting.

V. Surikov. *Menshikov at Beriozovo*. 1883. The Tretyakov Gallery

On 30 November 1729 the betrothal of the young couple took place and their wedding was appointed for 19 January 1730. However, on 6 January, the Day of the Theophany, the Emperor stood on the ice of the Moscow River in a nasty weather and caught cold. Three days later it was found that he had smallpox. The condition of the sick rapidly worsened and eventually, not regaining consciousness, he cried out the ominous phrase: "Harness horses to a sledge! I want to go to my sister!" and died. With the death of Peter II the direct male hereditary line of the Romanovs broke forever. During the last hours of the Emperor's life the Dolgorukys tried to push Princess Catherine to the throne with the help of a false testament but they failed – a session of the Supreme Secret Council proclaimed Anna Ioannovna, the Duchess of Courland, the new Empress of Russia.

ANNA

Anna Ioannovna
(28 January 1693, Moscow – 17 October 1740, St Petersburg),
the Empress from 19 January 1730

One of arguments put forward by Prince Dmitry Golitsyn, the head of the Supreme Secret Council, in favour of Anna Ioannovna's enthronement was the fact of her being the daughter of Ivan V, the half-brother and co-ruler of Peter the Great, and her descent in the maternal line from the ancient Russian Saltykov family. This argument overweighed, in Golitsyn's opinion, the chances of other candidates – the "not pedigree" Elizabeth, a daughter of Peter the Great and of the "common laundress" Catherine I, not to mention Prince Karl Peter Ulrich, who was in fact a foreigner – the son of the Duke of Holstein Karl Friedrich, born in Kiel, and Peter's daughter Anna, who died in 1728. After the death of his father in 1696 Tsarevna Anna lived, together with her mother and two sisters, the elder Yekaterina or Catherine (from 1716, the Duchess of Mecklenburg) and the younger Praskovya, in the suburban palace of Izmailovo that retained the patriarchal features of Moscow's everyday life. In 1708 Peter the Great prescribed Tsarina Praskovya Fiodorovna to move to St Petersburg with her daughters and married Anna to Friedrich Wilhelm, the Duke of Courland, there. The wedding took place on 31 October 1710. Anna widowed, however, almost immediately after her wedding – her young husband died on 9 January 1711, right before their depar-

H. Buchholz. *Portrait of Empress Anna Ioannovna.*
Last third of the 18th century. SM "Peterhof"

Empress Anna Ioannovna

Anna Ioannovna could hardly be called attractive –
she was a corpulent, manlike woman with a loud
shrilling voice and a heavy glance. Anna's entourage
did not like the Empress and were afraid of her.

Ernst Johann Biron (1690–1772), the Duke of Courland,
lover of Empress Anna Ioannovna

ture for Courland. Nevertheless Peter the Great did not allow the seventeen-year-old widow to remain at home and sent her to Courland as Russia's state interests demanded. Anna's life in the foreign land, amidst the hostile Courland nobility was difficult and sorrowful. Poverty, indefinite position and full dependence on the Tsar poisoned her life. Anna became intimate with Piotr Bestuzhev-Riumin, the Russian envoy to the Courland court, who supervised all affairs. This caused an irritation of Anna's peevish and domineering mother, Tsarina Praskovya, who did not like Anna and oppressed her in various ways to the end of her life in 1723. After Bestuzhev had been recalled to Russia in 1727, Anna's favourite became Ernst Johann Biron, and she retained her strong attachment to him throughout her life. In January 1730 Anna signed the restrictive "conditions" brought to her by members of the Supreme Secret Council. The "conditions" turned the autocracy into a monarchy limited by the council's officials. But on her arrival in Moscow at the beginning of February 1730 Anna established close ties with the circles of the nobility opposite to the council and on 25 February 1730 she took sudden measures equal to a coup: she tore up the conditions in public and reestablished the autocracy with the support of the guards.

Award cup of Empress
Anna Ioannovna.
Russia, Revel.
Craftsman: V. Adrian.
1736. SM "Peterhof"

J. Charlemagne. *Empress Anna Ioannovna Tearing the "Conditions" in 1730 at Moscow*

V. Jakobi. *Anna Ioannovna's Morning (Jesters at the Court of Anna Ioannovna)*

Her previous life, full of fears and humiliation, had a detrimental effect on the Empress's character. As regards her range of interests, Anna Ioannovna was a person of the transitive age – the pre-Petrine, old Muscovite values and notions lived in harmony in her soul with an interest in Western fashions, customs and pastimes. On becoming the Empress, she re-created the "Tsarina's Room" of her childhood with toadies, dwarfs and jesters typical of pre-Petrine Russia. At the same time Anna Ioannovna passionately loved the theatre and it was in her reign that the ballet appeared in Russia and the first opera was staged.

V. Surikov. *Empress Anna Ioannovna Shooting Reindeer in the Peterhof Temple*. 1900

In everyday life the Empress was a woman of petty interests, gossips and rumours remaining convinced that she was infallible as the Autocrat ("And if I want to do a favour to somebody – I am free in that!"). Her true passion was rifle and pistol shooting. But she displayed an almost complete indifference to state affairs preferring relaxation and pleasure to them. In her decrees she demanded her ministers "not to disturb Us for minor affairs." Anna Ioannovna mercilessly persecuted the enemies of her regime and her Secret Chancellery inspired freight.

Wedding of Jesters in the Ice Palace in the Reign of Anna Ioannovna

Fireworks on the occasion of the coronation of Empress Anna Ioannovna.
From the *Coronation Album*. 1730

The fate was favourable to Anna Ioannovna, as although she lacked a capacity to rule the state, the policies of her government were rather balanced and successful. The two wars (against Poland in 1734–35 and against Turkey in 1736–39) were successful and Russia strengthened her positions in Poland, Courland (she created Biron a duke there in 1737) and in the Black Sea area. Anna Ioannovna met the needs of the nobility by reducing the terms of their obligatory service and by granting some other privileges to them. Scaring the adherents of the Supreme Secret Council in Moscow, she moved back to St Petersburg at the beginning of 1732, which proved to be favourable for its further development.

An important political figure at the end of Anna's reign was the statesman and diplomat Artemy Volynsky (1689–1740)

Volynsky at the Session of the Council of Ministers

A patent signed by Empress Anna Ioannovna and Field Marshal Burchard Christoph von Münnich. 1733. SM "Peterhof"

Presentation ladle of Anna Ioannovna. Russia, Moscow. 1736. SM "Peterhof"

Unknown engraver. *Perspective View of the Neva in St Petersburg*. Mid-18th century.
SM "Peterhof". To the left, the Winter Palace of Empress Anna Ioannovna

The Empress surrounded herself with loyal people not engaged in "a venture of the Council members". Her entourage included both Russians and foreigners. Biron played a special role in Anna's reign. She did not part with Biron for a day – so great was her need for him. It is known that in 1728 Anna gave him a son, Karl Ernst, who was declared to be the youngest son of Biron and his wife. The child lived in the same apartments as the Empress. The end of her reign was darkened by executions. In that period the Empress displayed such qualities as suspicion, cruelty and vengeance. She avenged herself on the former leader of the Council members Dmitry Golitsyn as well as the Prince Dolgoruky family. It was not enough to her that they suffered for many years in exile at Beriozov. In 1738, a denunciatory report led to a new investigation as a result of which many members of the Dolgoruky family were executed in Novgorod and Tobolsk. In 1740 Artemy Volynsky, who did not please Biron, as well several of his companions, were falsely accused of conspiracy and treason. At the beginning of October 1740 the Empress's health suddenly shattered – she had an attack of gallstone disease – and soon she died. Shortly before her death Anna Ioannovna had declared an infant, Ioann (Ivan) Antonovich, the son of her niece Anna Leopoldovna, to be her successor on the throne with Duke Biron as the infant's regent.

IVAN VI

Ioann Antonovich,
(12 August 1740, St Petersburg – 4 July 1764, Schlüsselburg),
Emperor from 17 October 1740 to 25 November 1741)

Anxious about the succession, the childless (officially) Empress Anna Ioannovna issued in 1731 quite an unusual decree about the subjects' oath of allegiance to the successor to be appointed by her. This decree was to cut off an access to the throne for the descendants of Peter the Great and Catherine I and gave preference to the relations from "Ivan's line" of the Romanovs, for Anna supposed to hand over the throne to the still unborn child of her niece known as Anna Leopoldovna.

Tsar Ivan V and Tsarina Praskovya Fiodorovna had five daughters, of which three – Catherine, Anna and Praskovya – remained alive. Anna was married to the Duke of Courland, Catherine to Karl Leopold, the Duke of Mecklenburg-Schwerin, and Praskovya was in a morganatic marriage to General I. Mamonov. Catherine's marriage proved to be unhappy – Karl Leopold was a petty tyrant, a psychically unbalanced man, and at the beginning of the 1720s Catherine managed to break away, with some difficulty, from her tyrant of a husband and to return to Russia together with her daughter Elizabeth-Catherine-Christina born in 1718. With the accession of Anna Ioannovna their position at the court changed. After the oath of 1731 Anna Ioannovna's niece

Unknown artist. *Portrait of Ivan VI*. Early 1740s.
The Russian Museum

Ruler Anna Leopoldovna (1718–1746),
Ivan VI's mother

Anton Ulrich, Duke of Braunschweig-Luneburg
(1714–1774), Ivan VI's father

adopted the Orthodox confession of faith with the name of Anna Leopoldovna. The Empress took patronage of the girl and gave her a good education. At the same time a suitable party for the young girl began to be sought – a bridegroom from among the German princes. Their choice fell on Prince Anton Ulrich of Braunschweig-Lüneburg. In 1733 he came to Russia, but their marriage was postponed for a long time – the bride did not like the suitor. In 1739, at the insistence of the Empress, the wedding still took place, and on 2 August 1740 Anna Leopoldovna bore Prince Ivan Antonovich. It was to Ivan that Empress Anna Ioannovna bequeathed the throne after her death. But in real fact all power turned out to be in the hands of Biron made the regent. However, Field Marshal Burchard von Münnich, dissatisfied by Biron's primacy, made a secret agreement with the Tsar's parents and on 9 November 1740 overthrew the regent who was soon exiled. Anna Leopoldovna declared herself the ruler of Russia and her husband Prince Anton Ulrich was promoted to the rank of Generalissimo. Münnich, indignant with that, submitted an application for his resignation. Anna Leopoldovna, however, was a ruler, however, only for a short period. On 25 November 1741 the Tsesarevna Elizabeth Petrovna made a coup and dethroned Tsar Ivan VI. He was sent, together with his family, at first to Riga and then to Rannenburg in Voronezh Province. There the four-year-old Ivan was taken away for ever from his mother and under the name of Grigory brought to Kholmogory where an empty bishop's mansion was equipped as a prison for him and his family.

General Field Marsha
Count Burchard Christoph von Münnich
(1683–1767)

The Arrest of Biron

The regent Biron was overthrown by Münnich, brought to trial, accused
of high treason and sentenced to death, but pardoned and exiled to
Siberia (Tobolsk Province).

Before the beginning of January 1756 Ivan lived at Kholmogory, in the apartment isolated from the outer world; later he was taken to the Schlüsselburg and confined in a cell with a special guard. The authorities tried to keep the existence of Ivan VI in secret and the preservation of any documents, books or coins with his titles or regal representation were to be punished as a state crime. All the documents about the rule of Emperor Ivan VI were withdrawn from circulation and it was forbidden to mention his name both in official and private correspondence.

Emperor Ioann Antonovich
with the Lady-in-Waiting
Juliana von Mengden

Admittedly, this did not prevent people to tell in an undertone to one another about the young Tsar "suffering for the Orthodox faith". The prisoner's guards tried to depict him in their reports as a mad man, while Ivan, if suffering from confused articulation and stammering, was quite reasonable and knew that he was the Emperor. Elizabeth Petrovna once saw him and in March 1762 Peter III visited the prisoner. In the summer of 1763 Catherine the Great made a visit to Schlüsselburg, too, and after that she approved the new instruction for the interior guard. It prescribed to

F. Burov. *Peter III Visiting Ivan VI in the Schlüsselburg Fortress*. 1885. The Russian Museum

Vasily Mirovich by the Body of Ioann Antonovich on 5 July 1764 in the Schlüsselburg Fortress

kill the prisoner at the first ever attempt to free him. Soon, in the night of 5 August 1764, Second Lieutenant Vasily Mirovich persuaded the soldiers of his guard to rebel and tried to liberate Ivan VI. However, during the battle of Mirovich's detachment with the guard of the secret barracks the officers of the guard killed Ivan. Mirovich surrendered to the authorities but was not tortured contrary to the customs of the period and his relations were also not subjected to investigations. The above-mentioned instruction to the guard was concealed from the Investigating Committee conducting an official inquiry of Mirovich's case and that is why even at the sitting of the court there arose a debate about the lawfulness of the guardsmen's action as they killed a person of the royal blood. Eventually, unlike general expectation, Catherine the Great did not pardon Mirovich and he was beheaded in 1764. The body of Ivan VI was secretly buried in the Schlüsselburg Fortress. His death, like earlier the demise of Peter III, was very suitable for Catherine the Great.

Ivan VI's mother, Anna Leopoldovna, died at Kholmogory in 1746, after the birth of her son Alexei. This prince, like her other children (Yekaterina, Yelizaveta and Piotr) spent their lives almost entirely in the Kholmogory imprisonment. After spending in the prison more than thirty years and going blind, Prince Anton Ulrich died in 1774. His children in 1780 were taken to Denmark where they passed away one after another forgotten by everybody.

A. Tardieu. *Ivan VI*. 1780–1800.
SM "Peterhof"

ELIZABETH

Yelizaveta Petrovna,
(18 December 1709, Moscow – 25 December 1761, St Petersburg),
the Empress from 25 November 1741

Elizabeth, daughter of Peter the Great and Yekaterina Alexeyevna, was considered illegitimate, because her parents had not been married when she was born, although after their marriage in 1712 they legalized their children. Yekaterina's low origin was not forgotten and this point cast a shadow on her life until her accession. In the 1720s this factor became a formal reason for France's refusal to accept the proposal of Peter the Great to regard Elizabeth as the bride of Louis XV. But Elizabeth grew up in the atmosphere of love and warmth in her parents' home from her early years. The girl was a rare beauty. In 1721 she was officially declared to come of age, but for different reasons none of a whole series of suitors asking her hand in marriage did become her husband. After the death of Peter the Great nobody regarded her seriously as a probable successor; formally because of her unstable, thoughtless character and not very chaste conduct and in real fact because the powers-that-be stood up against a return to something like Peter's age with its reforms. However, with the accession of Ivan VI in 1740 the political significance of the Tsesarevna increased. The apparent weakness of the state power and incessantly changing favourites, foreigners by descent, caused an irritation of the guardsmen who remembered the age of Peter the Great.

C. Vanloo. *Portrait of Empress Elizabeth Petrovna*. 1760.
SM "Peterhof"

A reflection of the great Tsar's glory highlighted the figure of his daughter. People regarded her as a true successor of Peter's great accomplishments. Elizabeth used these moods in 1741 for inciting the guards to participate in the conspiracy organized by her closest associates with the support of the French and Swedish envoys.

On capturing power as a result of a night coup, Elizabeth became the Empress. But she was not really able to rule the country in a proper way and let many things to drift, shifting off

The personal predilections of Elizabeth, a true daughter of the Baroque Age, favourably influenced the development of an artistic taste at the court and in the capital. She patronized culture and did not money for the construction of magnificent palaces, which were erected by Francesco Bartolomeo Rastrelli and other architects.

P. Artemyev and N. Chelnakov from the original by M. Makhayev.
View of the Great Palace at Peterhof from the Gulf of Finland. 1761

Toilet set.
Royal Porcelain Manufactory,
Meissen, Germany. 1725–30.
SM "Peterhof"

a responsibility for affairs on her ministers and favourites. However, the direction of her policy under the slogan of the restoration of "sacred behests of Peter the Great" proved to be absolutely right. Some time had passed since Peter's age, offences were forgotten and passions calmed, so many people came to understand the true significance of Peter's era and felt an up-surge of national self-consciousness and pride for the past achievements. Peter's daughter on the throne was for many of them the guarantee and symbol of Russia's success attained in the age of her father. Besides, Elizabeth appeared as a shallow, dull-witted and naive beauty only to not very shrewd observers.

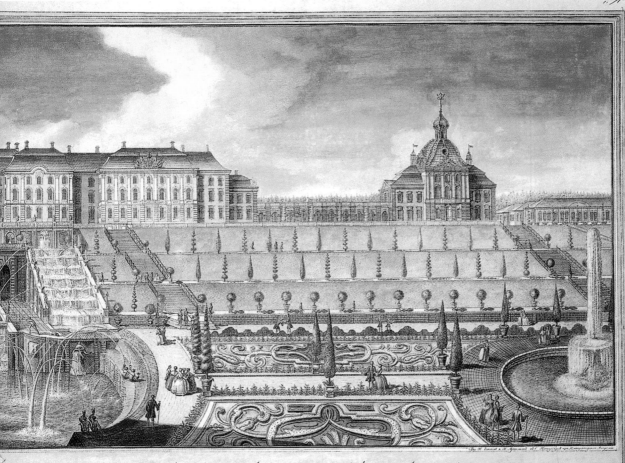

Peterhoff. Maison de Plaisance de Sa Maj.te Imp.le de toutes les Russies &c. &c. &c.
Située sur le Golfe de Finlande à trente Verstes de St Peterbourg.

In reality she was clever, ambitious, mistrustful and secretive. She remained the omnipotent autocrat and allowed nobody to overpower her – all final decisions, if not at once, were taken only by her. Remarkably, in the course of the coronation ceremony in Moscow on 25 April 1742 Elizabeth in a demonstrative way took the crown from the Metropolitan's hands and herself put it on her head stressing in this way that she owed her power only to herself. Catherine's policies betray predilections and caprices, but no haste or lack of consideration. Some inner "autocratic feeling" dictated her a cautious political conduct and enabled her to evade any risk. At that Elizabeth was in a permanent state of fear for her power and life; she was suspicious of any minute threat. For this reason Elizabeth never slept in the same place and, afraid of a night coup, used to keep awake all night resting in daytime.

Her reign saw a rapid economic growth in Russia. A demand for Russian steel in Europe attained 100% of its production, which promoted an industrial boom in the country. The liquidation of interior custom-houses in 1754 led to the invigoration of trade and growth of the state's incomes. The reign of Elizabeth appeared to be especially humane in comparison with other rul-

Presentation snuffbox with a portrait of
Empress Elizabeth Petrovna. Birmingham,
England. 1759. SM "Peterhof"
The snuffbox was made in memory of
the Russian army's victory over the Prussian
troops in the battle of Kunersdorf on
1 August 1759 in the course of the Seven-
Years' War.

ers. On her accession to the throne she took
an oath never to sign death sentences and for
twenty years nobody was executed in Russia.
In foreign policy Elizabeth stuck to the so-
called "system of Peter the Great" based on the
priority of fundamental imperial interests of
Russia. After the victory in the Russo-Swedish
War of 1741–43 Russia did not engage in any
war for thirteen years, but in 1756 declared
the Seven-Years' War on Prussia. Despite a
usual mess and thefts in the rear, the Russia
army succeeded to inflict three heavy blows
on the Prussian troops, and in the battle of
Kunersdorf Frederick II himself was defeated.
In 1758 Russia annexed East Prussia and in
1760 the Russian troops (together with the
Austrians) occupied Berlin.

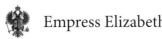

G.C. von Prenner.
Portrait of Empress Elizabeth Petrovna. 1754

Ivan Shuvalov (1727–1797),
lover of Empress Elizabeth

Shuvalov avoided to take an active part in
political life and preferred to devote himself
to science and arts. He was a passionate
art collector; his picture gallery and
the collection of ancient and West European
sculpture ranked with the best in Russia.

Alexei Razumovsky (1709–1771),
lover of Empress Elizabeth

Razumovsky was not an ambitious
man, but had a good sense of humour
and self-irony. Elizabeth granted him
"at parting" the rank of general-field
marshal and the Anichkov Palace.

As most of her contemporaries agreed, Elizabeth was an unusually beautiful woman. Tall, gracious, with a fair complexion, thin waist and lavish ash-grey hair, she was fascinating since her youth. She permanently looked for new fashionable dresses and ornaments, which were specially bought for her in Europe. In 1755 Moscow University was opened, in 1756 the first Russian public theatre began to work and in 1757 the Academy of arts was established. Officially Elizabeth remained unmarried. From 1731 on her lover was the former choir singer, the Ukrainian Cossack Alexei Razumovsky. It is likely that in 1742 they secretly married near Moscow. The consorts passionately loved each other, although rumour about their secret children, "the Tarakanovs", were just a fantasy of novelists. But in 1749 Elizabeth abandoned her "Olesha" for a new lover, Ivan Shuvalov, a well-educated youth, with a leaning towards art and sciences, a friend of Mikhail Lomonosov. Elizabeth lived with Shuvalov to the end of her life. An inevitable loss of her beauty over the years became for the Empress a reason for depression and even desperation. Her health, shattered by the immoderate way of living, drastically impaired. She died, not reaching fifty-three, on the festive day of the Nativity in 1761.

PETER III

Piotr Fiodorovich
(10 February 1728, Kiel, Germany – 6 July 1762,
Ropsha near St Petersburg),
the Emperor from 25 December 1761 to 28 June 1762

Peter III, the grandson of Peter the Great, was born in the Duchy of Holstein-Gottorp, whose head, Duke Karl Friedrich, had married Peter the Great's elder daughter, Anna, in 1725. After the birth of the boy named Karl Peter Ulrich, Anna died in May 1728. His father did not pay much attention to the child entirely trusting the prince's education to cruel and ignorant officers. Karl Friedrich also passed away in 1739 and the eleven-year-old prince became the duke. On her accession Empress Elizabeth, Karl Peter Ulrich's aunt, remembered about her nephew and summoned him to Russia. In 1742 the young Duke of Holstein adopted the Orthodox faith and was announced the successor with the name of Piotr Fiodorovich. He did not like Russia and missed his native Holstein. The grand duke behaved contrary to, and even in spite of, his aunt's desires. From his early years Piotr Fiodorovich revealed himself as a stubborn, silly person, hardly capable to rule the country. Capricious and infantile, he still remained neither angry nor cruel at that. He felt himself a stranger at the Russian court and, being rather cowardly, constantly lied and pretended because he knew that spies appointed by Elizabeth were watching secretly his every step.

Unknown artist. *Portrait of Grand Duke Piotr Fiodorovich, the Future Emperor Peter III.*
After 1743. SM "Peterhof"

Toy soldiers. Modelled about 1745. Royal Porcelain Manufactory, Meissen, Germany. SM "Peterhof"

Piotr Fiodorovich was fond of military amusements; toy soldiers, drilling military evolutions and the manual of arms.

Piotr Fiodorovich literally idolized the Prussian King Frederick II. During the Seven Years' War against Prussia he did not conceal his Pro-Prussian sympathies and on coming to the throne after the death of Elizabeth Petrovna he immediately concluded peace with Frederick II and at the beginning of 1762 entered a defensive union against Denmark, the age-old offender of Holstein. In the sphere of internal policy Peter III issued several important decrees. He forbade using the expression "The word and deed!" (employed by informers to attract the attention of the authorities), thus abolishing the institution that had terrorized society and provoked false denunciations since long ago. By another decree Peter III cancelled the terrific Secret Chancellery – the place of tortures and secret executions. In real fact, however, nobody abolished denunciations, just from that time denouncing information was to be given without loud crying and in a written form. As for the notorious Secret Chancellery, its functions passed to the Secret Expedition of the Senate. Several more liberal decrees also appeared in the reign of Peter III: a prohibition to persecute the Old Believers, the cancelling of a number of monopolies and a decree on the establishment of the State Bank. But the main act of Peter III was his Manifesto about the Freedom of the Gentry. It liberated members of the gentry from compulsory service for the first time, lent them a right to retire and a freedom to go abroad. This manifesto opened up important estate reforms marking the liberation of some part of Russian subjects from the domineering power of the autocracy and the state.

The Great Palace at Oranienbaum – the residence
of the Emperor Peter III

Grand Duke
Piotr Fiodorovich

A.R. Lisiewska. *Grand Duke Piotr Fiodorovich, Grand Duchess Yekaterina Alexeyevna and a Kalmyck Page*. 1756

The Murder of Peter III at Ropsha

Alexei Orlov (1737–1807)

Alexei Orlov, the junior brother of Grigory Orlov, played an especial role in the coup of 29 June. It was he who came to Peterhof and brought Catherine to St Petersburg, and after their arrival the mutiny began. Later he delivered the overthrown Emperor Peter III Ropsha, where he was taken into custody in the palace. Alexei Orlov participated in Peter's murder – he narrated about that in his letters to Catherine II from Ropsha.

The Ropsha Palace

But from the first days of his rule Peter III incited the gentry and the Guards against himself. His plan of an absurd campaign to Denmark, a demonstrative neglect of Russia's traditions and customs, and an introduction of the Prussian uniform in the army – all that irritated society. Peter's clever and ambitions wife, Empress Yekaterina Alexeyevna, skilfully employed these negative moods. Together with her lover Grigory Orlov, his brothers and guards she arranged a conspiracy and on 28 June 1762 made a coup to capture the throne. The weak-willed Peter III surrendered to the mercy of the victorious group and abdicated. He was taken to the Ropsha estate and strangled there by the Empress's associates.

CATHERINE II

Yekaterina Alexeyevna, called "the Great"
(21 April 1729, Stettin – 6 November 1796, St Petersburg),
the Empress-Consort from 25 December 1761,
the Autocratic Empress from 28 June 1762

In 1745 the heir to the throne Piotr Fiodorovich married, at the behest of Empress Elizabeth, Princess Sophie Friederike Augusta of Anhalt-Zerbst, who became, on her conversion to Orthodoxy, Yekaterina Alexeyevna or Catherine. From the first years of her life in Russia, where she came in February 1744 at the invitation of the Russian Empress, Catherine read much and according to a definite programme that might be called her "home university". She was unhappy with her husband and did not like him. Catherine was an ambitious young lady aspiring to ascend to the throne. Endowed with a good mind, tact and wit, she established important connections in high society and in the guard. The plot led by her lover Grigory Orlov and his four brothers, officers of the Guard, proved to be successful. Early in the morning on 28 June 1762 Catherine secretly left Peterhof, where the court stayed, for St Petersburg, and the Orlov brothers incited the Guard to revolt that morning. The troops went out into the streets of the capital and greeted Catherine. A service was held in the Kazan Cathedral and the oath of allegiance to the new Sovereign was made. After that the troops with Catherine at their head marched towards Peterhof. Peter III was arrested and imprisoned at Ropsha to be soon killed.

Unknown Russian artist. *Portrait of Empress Catherine the Great as a Legislatress in the Temple of Themis.*
Last quarter of the 18th century. SM "Peterhof"

V. Ericksen. *Equestrian Portrait of Catherine the Great*. 1762. SM "Peterhof"

This well-known portrait of Catherine the Great was painted soon after the state coup. Catherine, already proclaimed Empress in St Petersburg, is depicted in the uniform of a Colonel of the Preobrazhensky Regiment, in a cocked hat, with a sword in her hand, on her favourite horse Brilliant, at the start of her march to Peterhof, against Peter III.

After seizing power Catherine used every means to strengthen her position on the throne. She generously awarded the participants in the revolt, but still did her best to dissociate herself from them. Her affectionate conduct and well-wishing to everybody calmed society, while her intellect and innate dignity helped her become the true Sovereign. The final episode of this recognition was the luxurious coronation of Catherine the Great in September 1763 in Moscow.

Grigory Orlov (1734–1783)
Guard officer and an important figure in the coup that brought Catherine to the peak of power.

J. Kaestner. *Departure of Empress Yekaterina Alexeyevna from Peterhof on the Day of Her Elevation to the Throne*. 1762-63. SM "Peterhof"

Here, at Peterhof, by the entrance to the Upper Gardens, Alexei Orlov waited for Catherine, so as to bring her to St Petersburg and proclaim Empress of Russia Catherine II.

J. Kaestner. *Empress Catherine the Great at the Steps of the Church of the Mother of God of Kazan*. 1762–63. SM "Peterhof"

Voltaire (real name François Marie Arouet, 1694–1778)

He was an idol of several generations in the eighteenth century. A brilliant philosopher with a sharp, caustic pen, he wrote poems, plays, prose and scholarly treatises. His jokes were widespread by words of mouth, his satirical works brought him the fame of a derisive writer overthrowing authorities and an atheist.

Unknown artist. *Portrait of Catherine the Great Holding the Text of Her "Instructions"*. Late 1760s–1770s

Manuscript of the book *Russian Apothegmata, or an Excerpt from the Instruction Given by the Commission Compiling a Project for the New Code of Laws*. 18th century. The title page depicts the monogram of Catherine the Great and a bee-hive, the favourite symbol of the Russian Empress.

Catherine liked French literature and her idol was Voltaire. On her accession she began to correspond with him, D'Alambert and other prominent Enlighteners. Her contacts with these philosophers proved to be important for the formation of Catherine's personality as a state figure. Many ideas of the Enlightenment became part of her programme of reforms and were realized in laws.

It was in Catherine's reign that notions of the rights of estates appeared in Russia and some basic elements of civic society were laid down. But Catherine still remained the Autocrat with no restrictions to her power and the first reforms of the 1760s even increased this power. At that time the Senate was transformed, the Hetmanship was abolished in the Ukraine; church lands were secularized and became the property of the state. Almost a million of monastery peasants became free.

In 1767 Catherine set up the Commission for the Compilation of the New Code (codex of laws). Deputies representing the gentry, merchants and the peasantry gathered from the entire country to its sessions. Catherine wrote for the Commission her famous *Instruction*, in which she condemned selfdom and tortures and expressed the idea of the primacy of law in social life. *The Instruction* became a basis for Catherine's estate and other reforms.

Samovar with the monogram of Catherine the Great. Russia. 1770s–1780s. SM "Peterhof"

Cup of Catherine the Great. Imperial Porcelain Factory, St Petersburg, Russia. 1770s. SM "Peterhof"

J.-B. Nini. *Portrait of Catherine the Great.*
1770s. SM "Peterhof"

Charter of Catherine the Great. 1790

Snuffbox. Russia, St Petersburg.
1760s. SM "Peterhof"

Snuffbox. Paris, France. 1780s.
SM "Peterhof"

Snuffbox. Imperial Porcelain Factory,
St Petersburg, Russia. 1750s.
SM "Peterhof"

Catherine the Great dreamed to assert law and order in Russia by creating such an estate system, in which each subject would enjoy unalienable rights and privileges protected by laws. The new order was based on the transformations of the court and local government as well as on the publication of the Charter to the Gentry and of the Charter to the Cities (1785). The law provided the gentry and urban dwell-

Fan of Empress Catherine the Great.
France. 1780–96. SM "Peterhof"

ers with wide rights for self-government and the estate law court. At the same time important decrees were taken about the abolishment of corporal punishment for members of the gentry and merchants, about "free" printing companies (1783) and other laws.

To the very end of her life Catherine worked at the creation of the "constitution" understanding this term as a codex of rights of different classes, including the peasantry. All of them were guaranteed a right for life, private safety, health, presumption of being non-guilty and a right for legal defence. It was supposed to proclaim a freedom of consciousness and it was forbidden to punish "for people's thoughts and words".

It was the first time that Russian people could hear from their Sovereign not threats but calls to make good: "Don't do to another what you cannot bear yourself… Not only do no harm, but do good if you can… Help one another in doing good, lead a blind man, give a shelter to a homeless man, bring water to him that is thirsty… have mercy to a drowning man, stretch out your hand to help a falling man… Blessed is he who cares for cattle, too, and even if your enemy's animal is stumbling, help it rise to its feet… Show the way to him who lost his path." All this shows a pattern of Catherine's thoughts, her sincere and kind desire to improve the ways of society. No Sovereign had ever addressed such humanistic appeals to his or her subjects.

Uniform dress of Empress Catherine the Great as an officer of the Life Guards Preobrazhensky Regiment. St Petersburg, Russia. 1780s. SM "Peterhof"

Shoes of Catherine the Great. France (?). 1770s. SM "Peterhof"

Empress Catherine II

The rebel Yemelyan Pugachev
(1740/1742–1775), who posed as the saved
Emperor Peter III

Catherine's policy inside the country was based on a striving to convert Russia into "a legislative monarchy", to compile a system of laws that would guarantee a protection from arbitrariness, corruption and poverty to all her subjects. The idea of attaining "universal good" was then the most popular political dream. The existence of serfdom remained the most acute problem. Catherine understood that the extension of the rights of the nobility and the merchant class would not prove to be effective with the existence of serfdom. But she feared to touch this theme, troublesome for the majority of the gentry having serfs – she highly valued her power and would not like to risk it for the sake of the abolishment of serfdom. Meanwhile the lack of laws limiting the oppression of peasants impaired the situation. In 1773 an immense revolt led by the Don Cossack Yemelyan Pugachev broke out. Later Catherine would call it a "horror of the eighteenth century'. The rebels destroyed the estates of landlords, tortured and killed members of the gentry, including women and children. The revolt spread over large territories. Catherine was afraid that the mutiny would reach the central regions and Moscow. It took great efforts to suppress the revolt; Pugachev was captured, brought to Moscow and executed in January 1775.

F. Durfeldt from the original by F. I. Gatterberger(?). *Russian Popular Games in a Street.* 1790

80

Unknown engraver. *The Triumph of Empress Catherine the Great*.
1792. SM "Peterhof"

This allegorical composition with gods and genii celebrates the Empress.

A. Kazachinsky from a drawing by J.-L. de Velly and
M. Makhayev. *Catherine the Great Receiving the Turkish
Ambassador on 14 October 1764 in the Winter Palace*. 1796

Army commander, Generalissimo of the Russian
troops Alexander Suvorov (1730–1800)

In the reign of Catherine the Great the borders of the Empire were extended both to the south and west. In the course of two wars against Turkey (1768–74 and 1787–91) Russia annexed the Crimea and consolidated its position on the coastlands of the Black Sea where new cities and towns were founded. These wars revealed the military genius of Piotr Rumiantsev, Alexander Suvorov and Fiodor Ushakov. Russia's naval successes proved to be no less outstanding. In 1770 the Russian fleet commanded by Alexei Orlov made an expedition from the Baltic Sea to the Mediterranean and succeeded in driving the Turkish Navy into the Chesme Bay (Greece) and burning down its ships there. That was a brilliant victory, and a medal was struck in its honour depicting the burning Turkish Fleet and inscribed: *It was*. Another major success of the Russian State was the foundation of Sevastopol, the chief naval base at the Black Sea, in the Crimea in 1783.

J.Ph. Hackert. *The Burning of the Turkish Fleet in the Chesme Bay*. 1772. SM "Peterhof"

The newly built Black Sea Navy under the command of Admiral Ushakov won several victories over the Turkish Fleet and established Russia's dominance on the Black Sea. As a result of the three partitions of Poland (1772, 1793, 1795) Russia, together with Austria and Prussia, captured a significant part of the lands formerly owned by the Rheczpospolita. In the war against Sweden (1788–90) Russia defended its former territorial gains in the Baltic area.

In the war against revolutionary France that began after 1789 Russia joined the coalition of European monarchic states, but Catherine skilfully maneuvered not to enter the war against the Republicans. At first she even rejoiced at the misfortunes of the haughty Bourbons, but after the murder of Louis XVI she began to beware of the penetration of the "revolutionary plaque" to Russia. This led to making the regime within the state more severe.

Commander-in-Chief of the Russian Navy in the Russo-Turkish War of 1768–74 Alexei Orlov (1737–1807)

Lover of Empress Catherine the Great
Grigory Potemkin (1739–1791)

A considerable phase in Catherine's reign was associated with the activities of Grigory Potemkin, who became her lover about 1744 (and later probably her secret husband). Potemkin was a man of exceptional talents. Under his supervision new towns such as Kherson, Sevastopol, Odessa and Nikolaev were built in the bare southern steppes in the 1780s; thousands of Russian peasants constructed fortresses, factories, canals and shipyards and planted forests. The streams of Russian, Ukrainian and German colonists rushed to Novorussia (as Russia's new possessions were called) to cultivate the extremely rich steppe lands. All that was accomplished thanks to the will, mind and energy of Potemkin who enjoyed the Empress's trust. He had a very unusual character and seemed to be a strange man to many people, but all recognized his genius as a statesman.

Unknown artist. *Allegory of Travel of Catherine the Great Around the South of the Russian Empire in 1787*. Late 18th – early 19th century

Alexander Lanskoi
(1758–1784)

Alexander
Dmitriyev-Mamonov
(1758–1803)

Platon Zubov
(1767–1822)

Stanislaw August
Poniatowski
(1732–1798),
King of Poland
in 1764–95

Catherine was unhappy in her private life.
A sensuous woman, she could not live, as
she herself admitted, without love. But
she was unlucky with her partners, be
it her husband Peter III, Grigory Orlov,
Grigory Potemkin or numerous younger
lovers, as they did not meet the high
standards set by her. Throughout her life
Catherine was looking for an akin soul,
for a man capable to comprehend and
appreciate her personality. But she could
not find her match and over the years her
searches resulted in romances with young
cavaliers, in a hope to educate one of
them into an ideal man she was looking
for. So she wrote about her last favourite
Platon Zubov: "I do a good service to
the state by educating young people."

Empress
Catherine
the Great

J. Pulmann. *Portrait of Grand Duke Pavel Petrovich.*
1782–87

The relations of Catherine the Great with her son, Grand Duke Pavel Petrovich, developed unevenly and with difficulty. After his birth Pavel was taken away from his mother to be educated in the apartments of Empress Elizabeth, so he did not have any filial feelings. The delicate circumstances of Catherine's ascend to power and an apparent desire of the circle led by the successor's tutor, Nikolai Panin, to see the grand duke on the throne, made him a rival in the eyes of his mother and caused the Empress's desire to move him as far away from the throne as possible. She did not allow Pavel Petrovich to participate in state affairs, did not forbid her lovers to offend her son and humiliate him and herself commented very negatively on his abilities and even did not conceal that from other people. Catherine's son paid her in his own coin. Brief periods of their friendly relations were succeeded by years of their silent, official coolness, mutual suspicion and mistrust. After Grand Duke Pavel Petrovich and Maria Fiodorovna had given birth to a son, Alexander, in 1777, Catherine took her grandson away from his parents and began to educate the child herself with an aim in view to prepare him as her worthy successor. She did the same, to the despair of Pavel and Maria after the birth of their second son, Konstantin. Alexander

and Konstantin were educated according to a special program compiled by the Empress herself. When Catherine was writing the program, she imagined Pavel standing before her eyes: a sickly and weak boy, he was spoiled by a bad, female education in the stale apartments of Empress Elizabeth and grew up into a wick-willed, nervous and envious man. Alexander, as Catherine thought, would become a different stock: hardened, sleeping in an open air, in light clothes, this young Spartan would divide his time between energetic physical exercises and deep studies with a clever and well-educated tutor. To this position she appointed the Swiss republican Frédéric César de La Harpe. Here are some excerpts from the *Instructions on the Education of Grandsons* written by Catherine in the spring of 1783: To prevent and forbid Their Highnesses to do harm to themselves or human beings and hence not to beat or scold in their presence and not to allow them to beat, pinch or scold a man or an animal and not to inflict any pain or harm. Lie should be presented to them as a disgraceful thing entailing contempt and mistrust of all people... The main emphasis in the children's instruction should be on love for one's neighbour (do not do to another what you don't want to be done to you), on a general kindness to the human being, in a benevolent attitude to all people, in a tender and tolerant treatment of anybody, in an incessant good behaviour, in pure and noble heart, in the elimination of hot temper, unfounded misgiving, fear and suspicion." The boys' life passed close to their grandmother, who learned the alphabet with them, played, travelled and walked around. Catherine was especially satisfied with Alexander: "I am fond of him and if possible, I would keep this boy near me throughout my life" (from her letter to Grimm of 30 May 1779). She called Alexander "the delight of my heart". Gradually it became clear to many people, what this wholehearted love would lead to. Pavel Petrovich and his adherents were especially disturbed when Catherine married her 16-year-old grandson to the 14-year-old Princess Louise of Baden (Yelizaveta Alexeyevna). This confirmed the rumour about the Empress's firm intention to bequeath the throne "passing" her unloved son right to her grandson, who became after his marriage the head of his own family and a rightful man. Catherine's will had not reached us, but rumours about her intention were quite persistent. In August 1792 she wrote to Grimm, probably continuing their previous discussion by correspondence: "Listen, why should we hurry with the coronation? This is not to my taste. Solomon said: *To every thing there is a season*. At first we shall marry Alexander

Catherine the Great with her grandsons –
Grand Dukes Alexander and Konstantin

Grand Duke Alexander Pavlovich

and then, over the time, we shall crown him as Tsar with great celebrations and all kinds of popular festivities. Everything will be brilliant and majestic. Oh, how happy he will be and how others will be happy with him!" All that was written as though Pavel Petrovich had died a long time ago. In September 1791 Catherine informed Grimm again that in case a revolution would break out in Europe, a tyrant would appear and enslave it, but "that will not happen in my reign and, I hope, in the reign of Alexander." The reign of Paul I seemed not to be expected. But she thought about his fate, too. Let us look into Catherine's note about the tragic conflict of Peter the Great with Tsarevich Alexei, who was deprived of his right to succeed the throne. It seems to be just a usual historical note, nothing more. One should, however, pay attention to Catherine's sincere conviction that Peter was right: "It must be admitted that the parent who has to reject his breed for the sake of the common cause is unlucky. The autocratic and parental power is coupled here. So I presume that the wisdom of the Sovereign Peter the Great is undoubted, he had the greatest reasons to renounce his unthankful, disobedient and incapable son. The latter was filled with hate, anger and sole envy against him, he sought in his father's actions for specks of dust in a basket of good, he listened to flatterers and divided the truth from his ears and nothing could please him as much as abusing and saying bad things about his glorious father..."

Her son Alexei, born by Grigory Orlov in 1762 (later known under the name of Count Bobrinsky), also did not become close to her. For many years he was educated in the family of the Chief Wardrobe Master V. Shkurin and that could not but affect his development. Catherine felt no motherly feelings to him and even did not see her son for many years. Bobrinsky was given to the Cadet Corps, and upon graduation was sent to study abroad. But he led a wild life and for six years would not obey Catherine's order to return to his homeland. On his return Bobrinsky was put under house arrest on his estate. After his succession Paul I summoned him to St Petersburg, called him his brother and bestowed the rank of general upon him, but Bobrinsky did not want to serve and soon went back to his estate where he spent his time in comfort and idleness until his death in 1813.

Unknown artist. *Portrait of Empress Catherine the Great.* Late third of the 18th century. SM "Peterhof"

C. Christineck. *Alexei Bobrinsky.* 1769

The poet Gavriil Derzhavin (1743–1816), State-Secretary in the reign of Empress Catherine the Great

Architect Alexander Kokorinov (1726–1772), Rector of the Imperial Academy of Arts from 1769

The Catherine age saw outstanding accomplishments in the arts. St Petersburg as well as Moscow and other cities were adorned with majestic buildings in the style of Classicism created by the architects Jean-Baptiste Vallin de La Mothe, Alexander Kokorinov, Yury Velten, Antonio Rinaldi, Mikhail Kazakov, Vasily Bazhenov, Charles Cameron, etc. Fedot Shubin's chisel "enlivened" cold marble in his sculptural portraits, and the "Bronze Horseman", a monument to Peter the Great designed by Etienne Maurice Falconet and unveiled in 1782, strikes people to this day by the powerful thrust of the regal rider. Dmitry Levitsky with his famous portraits of the Smolny Institute girls, Fiodor Rokotov, Vladimir Borovikovsky and Nikolai Argunov reigned supreme in painting. The best European plays and operas were staged in both state-owned and serf theatres (there were 170 of them!). Plays by Alexander Sumarokov, Denis Fonvisin and Vasily Kapnist were also performed and music by Dmitry Bortniansky and Maxim Berezovsky could be heard; majestic odes by Gavriil Derzhavin were recited.

The ideas of Enlightenment and the power of knowledge in the fight against prejudices led the Empress to a conviction that it was necessary to "grow up a new man", well-educated, law-abiding and laborious. The ideologist of the new pedagogical principles was one of Catherine's closest associates, Ivan Betskoi. His most famous initiative was the establishment of the Imperial Society for Girls of Noble Birth at the Smolny Convent (1764), which provided an excellent education for young noble girls. Young girls of the third estate could study at the newly founded institute attached to the New Maiden Convent in St Petersburg. In general, the network of foundling hospitals – a sort of boarding schools for orphans and foundlings – was supposed to yield to Russia the "third estate" of businessmen, merchants and craftsmen. One could also receive education in private or "free" schools as well as in boarding schools. There were nearly fifty of them in St Petersburg in 1784.

The last years of Catherine's reign were marked by the weakening of her creative capacity and general stagnation in social life.

Yekaterina Dashkova (1745–1810)

Dashkova occupied a place apart in the history of Russian culture. She belonged to the circle of people close to Catherine, took part in the conspiracy and the coup of 1762. But later her relations with the Empress grew worse. Dashkova went abroad, travelled much and made the acquaintance of the French Enlighteners, in particular Voltaire. In 1783 Catherine appointed Dashkova the Director of the Academy of Sciences. A clever and resolute woman, Dashkova managed to improve the work of the Academy. In the same year a new establishment, the Russian Academy, was organized upon her initiative which engaged, unlike the "large"

Academy, to the humanities and focused on the problems of the Russian language. Its building stands to this day on Vasilyevsky Island and each connoisseur of the Russian language would take off his hat passing it. Dashkova set up to the Russian Academy a complex task:

"To extol the Russian word, to gather it into a single whole, to show its space, abundance and beauty, to set unalterable rules for it, to reveal the brevity and significance of its sayings and to explore its deep antiquity." She initiated the compilation of *Dictionary of the Russian Academy* and edited *The Collocutor of the Lovers of the Russian Word*. Derzhavin, Fonvizin and Kniazhnin published their works in this journal, and Catherine herself contributed to this edition. At the same time, largely thanks to Dashkova, an infatuation of intellectuals with the Russian language and history began. The first dictionary was compiled merely within six years and it is impossible to imagine the existence of the Russian language without it. But towards the end of Catherine's age things were going not very well for Dashkova. Even the slightest hint about a revolution or republic scared the Empress, who had been frightened by the French Revolution.

The Academy published the play *Vadim of Novgorod*, which eulogized a republican freedom. Catherine's anger was directed against Dashkova, who supervised the book-publishing program of the Academy of Science. This led to Dashkova's retirement. She devoted the last years of her life to writing memoirs – the famous *Notes of Princess Dashkova*.

A. Melnikov. *The Unveiling of the Monument to Peter the Great on Senate Square in St Petersburg*. 1782

The picture shows the most important monument of the Catherine Age that came to be known as *The Bronze Horseman* and immediately grew into a symbol of St Petersburg. Its creator was the sculptor Etienne Maurice Falconet. The unveiling of the monument took place in the summer of 1782 and was arranged as a triumph of the Empire and resembled a grand-scale theatrical performance.

ЕКАТЕРИНА ВТОРАЯ.

N. Utkin from the original by V. Borovikovsky.
Empress Catherine the Great. 1827. SM "Peterhof"

The outbreak of the French Revolution frightened the Empress and she began to reveal intolerance and conservatism that had not been characteristic of her before. The victims of her anger were Alexander Radishchev, the author of *A Travel from St Petersburg to Moscow*, the publisher and journalist Nikolai Novikov and the playwright Yakov Kniazhnin. The Empress's turn to reaction was encouraged by her last favourite, Platon Zubov.

Alexander Radishchev
(1749–1802)

Formerly Catherine had repeatedly written how she would be dying among her friends, to the sounds of tender music. But death overtook her in a narrow passage between two rooms of the Winter Palace. She had a bad stroke and several servants took great efforts to carry the heavy body of the Empress from the narrow passage and put her on the mattress laid on the floor. She died there several hours later not recovering her consciousness. Catherine the Great did not leave her testament, although there is a surmise that she did write it and according to the will the throne was to pass not to her son Paul but to her favourite grandson Alexander. However, this will is said to fall into Paul's hands and be burnt it in a fireplace.

S. Shchedrin. *The Grand Pond at Tsarkoye Selo.* 1777

PAUL I

Pavel Petrovich
(20 September 1754, St Petersburg – 11 March 1801, St Petersburg),
Emperor from 6 November 1796

Paul was born into the family of the heir to the throne Piotr Fiodorovich (the future Peter III) and Yekaterina Alexeyevna (later Catherine II). He grew up as a shy and well-developed boy, inclined to romantic, noble impulses and knightly deeds. However, his life was not successful. Although being the heir to the throne, he did not enjoy any influence. Paul's relations with his mother were strained; her favourites humiliated him and he suffered from court intrigues and shadowing. Paul's relations with his mother acquired a special touch of drama owing to the rumour spread by gossips that he was not the son of Peter III, but just the fruit of his mother's sinful love to Sergei Saltykov. Catherine herself neither confirmed this rumour in her memoirs nor rejected it. Paul's first early marriage also proved to be unhappy – his wife Natalia Alexeyevna (Auguste Wilhelmine, Princess of Hesse-Darmstadt) was unfaithful to her husband with his friend Alexei Razumovsky and in 1776 died in childbirth. Paul, though, soon found his happiness in a new marriage, to Maria Fiodorovna, who gave him numerous children.

Unknown painter from the original by V. Borovikovsky.
Portrait of Emperor Paul I. Early 19th century.
SM "Pavlovsk"

Paul was left out of things until forty-two. Over the years the heir's starry-eyed impulses and dreams about his lofty designation vanished leaving the feelings of suspicion and powerless fury, a desire to "do away with the debauchery of the court" and "to establish order" in society. Paul implemented these ideas on his estate at Gatchina. There, encircled by faithful people, he felt himself out of danger and built a small "regular kingdom", the experience which he applied, on his succession, to the entire country.

Paul I was a convinced enemy of the methods of ruling used by Catherine the Great and an admirer of Frederick II. This disposition of mind became apparent from the very first days of his reign when he began to struggle with the "depravity" of the Guards, army and government by means of severe discipline and by punishing even for negligent faults. Policemen fiercely attacked those passers-by that ignored decrees forbidding to wear some kinds of clothes like round "French" hats. The army had its uniform changed and its re-education began at once ac-

First wife of Grand Duke
Pavel Petrovich,
Princess Wilhelmine-Louise
of Hesse-Darmstadt, from 1773,
Natalia Alexeyevna
(1755–1776)

Second wife of Grand Duke Pavel Petrovich, Princess Sophie Dorothea of Württemberg-Stuttgart, from 1776, Maria Fiodorovna (1759–1828)

M.F. Quadal. *The Coronation of Paul I and Maria Fiodorovna on 5 April 1797 in the Assumption Cathedral in Moscow*

G. Sergeyev. *Military Parade at Gatchina*. 1798

Unknown painter from the original by J.-B. Lampi. *Emperor Paul I with His Suite*. Late 18th century

Paul I and his entourage
in Prussian military uniform

cording to the new, Prussian system of ruthless discipline and line drilling favoured by Paul. The usual ceremony of the changing of the guard turned into an important state affair with the obligatory participation of the Emperor and the successor. The spirit of soldiery was hovering over the capital. In 1798 Paul abolished the Letter Patents granted to the gentry and to cities and introduced corporal punishments again. His subjects heard many surprising decrees such as on the prohibition of importing "all kinds of books in whatever language" and of any sheets of music, about the clothing of nearly all printing-houses. In 1800 Paul issued a special decree that one was allowed to applaud in the theatre only when the Sovereign did so, etc. On the day of his coronation, 5 April 1797, Paul I passed a decree of succession, which rigidly regulated the succession primarily according to the male linear descent rather than at the monarch's will as it had sometimes occurred in the past. This decree would remain valid throughout the nineteenth century. Simultaneously the *Statute of the Imperial Family* was published, which fixed the principles of seniority in the now large Imperial family as well as the principles of provision of its members by means of the so-called Department of Crown Domain.

G. Kügelchen. *Portrait of Emperor Alexander I*. 1801–03. SM "Peterhof"

A.-F. Lagrenée. *Portrait of Grand Duchess Yelena Pavlovna*. 1820s. SM "Peterhof"

In 1776 Grand Duke Pavel Petrovich married Sophie Dorothea Auguste Louise, Princess of Württemberg, who became known in Russian history as Maria Fiodorovna. The young couple led a merry and quiet life. Pavel's wife was healthy, beautiful and solicitous. She turned out to be a good mother and gave birth to ten children, of which only one died in early childhood. The first child was Alexander (1777–1825), followed by Konstantin (1779–1731). After that for thirteen years, to her husband's discontent, she gave birth only to girls: Alexandra (1783–1801), Yelena (1784–1803), Maria (1786–1859), Yekaterina (1788–1818), Olga (1792–1795) and Anna (1795–1865). And only at the end of their marriage two boys were born: Nikolai (1796–1855) and Mikhail (1798–1849).

A. Taurel from the original by J.B. van der Hulst. *Portrait of Grand Duchess Anna Pavlovna*. 1846. SM "Peterhof"

A. Rockstuhl. *Portrait of Grand Duke Mikhail Pavlovich*. 1819. SM "Peterhof"

G. Sergeyev. *The Carp Pond at Gatchina*. 1798

Unknown artist. *The genealogical tree of Emperor Paul I.* 1798

For a long time the family of Pavel and Maria lived in Gatchina presented by Catherine to her son in 1783. As early as the autumn of the same year Pavel and Maria moved to Gatchina and began to name themselves "Gatchina landlords". This is how Pavel's long Gatchina epic began. He started to reconstruct the estate and lay out gardens in the English style. The consorts had a small court there and used to arrange musical parties and festivities. They enjoyed especial pleasure from amateurish performances staged in the small theatre of the palace. Yekaterina Nelidova, who later became Pavel's lover, performed leading female parts. The successor himself did not appear on the stage, but took an active participation in the preparation of the performances. Maria Fiodorovna had an artistic talent – she was fond of music, had a good command of drawing, carved medals on bone and stone and could operate a lathe. Some elegant pieces made by her have reached our days.

Snuffbox with portraits of Grand Duke Pavel Petrovich and his wife Maria Fiodorovna. Moscow, Russia. 1796.
SM "Peterhof"

The management of the large economic sector at Gatchina supervised by Maria Fiodorovna was quite bothersome. Dairies, cattle-yards and stables catered for the needs of the small courtyard and were perfectly organized. Maria Fiodorovna seemed to be an outsider in court society occupied with rumours, intrigues and philandering. She was honest, frank and faithful to her husband. She loved him and devoted all her time to the education of their children. Catherine was slightly irritated with that and wrote with a touch of irony that Pavel's daughters would be like their mother: "Keep yourself straightly, take care of your waist and complexion, eat for four, reasonably choose books for reading and eventually they will grow up excellent citizens for any country." Although Maria naturally was not endowed with Catherine's mind and will, she was a praiseworthy person, an elegant and luxurious woman and a good wife.

Unknown artist. *Portrait of Emperor Paul I*. Late 18th century. SM "Peterhof"

Pavlovsk became one of favourite places of Grand Duke Pavel Petrovich and Grand Duchess Maria Fiodorovna. Before 1777 there were only two hunting lodges in this area, "Krik" and Krak", for lovers of duck hunting. When Catherine presented the surrounding lands to her son, a new name, Pavlovskoye (later changed for Pavlovsk), appeared. Two wooden buildings, Paullust (Pavel's Amusement) and Marienthal (Maria's Valley) were built at first. Later the toy fortress Bip was put up. Simultaneously with the erection of the buildings work on the creation of the park began, too: there appeared cuttings, pavilions, statues and flowerbeds. In 1779 the construction of the Great Palace began. Its designer Charles Cameron, an architect invited from England, was a great aesthete and a connoisseur of

ancient literature and architecture. The owners liked his main idea – to create an austere ancient building amidst virginal nature. Later wings were added, which skirted in a semi-circle a vast courtyard, in the centre of which stood a monument to Peter the Great. This courtyard was used for parades and military exercises so much loved by Paul I.

It is from a wide avenue of clipped lime-trees running from the courtyard that the Pavlovsk Park with numerous crossing and meeting avenues begins. Near the palace, like at Gatchina, was laid out Her Majesty's Own Garden in the French style, which was accessible to Maria Fiodorovna directly from her private apartments. The dwelling apartments of the palace were divided into two sections, one of them belonging to Maria and the other to Pavel. With all stylistic unity of the interiors each section had some specific features: in the "male" part prevailed symbols of war and various military attributes that could be seen everywhere, whereas in the "female" part dominated artistic symbols and flowers. The specific feature of the palace was in that its furniture was produced individually, from sketches by the architects who were building or designing its halls and

rooms. Once put on a definite place, a chair or a cupboard was associated with this place forever – it would look un-natural in a different position. All that endows Pavlovsk with a sense of especial harmony that has made it famous all over the world.

Pavel was a biased owner. Not infre-quently he had bitter arguments with Cameron and eventually the Tsesarevich dismissed the architect – so different were their aesthetic positions. The style of Vincenzo Brenna who replaced Cam-eron was more suitable to Pavel's taste. Characteristic of Cameron was English refinement, restraint and lyricism, where-as Brenna introduced a touch of formal crudeness and demonstrative emphasis on wealth, so appreciated by the owner. Some other eminent architects, such as Giacomo Quarenghi, Jean-Baptiste Thom-as de Thomon, Carlo Rossi and Andrei Voronikhin, also worked at Pavlovsk.

The park was laid out with a great ingenuity and its creators took into consideration the picturesque local-ity in the flood-lands of the Slavianka River. One section of the park is typically French, regular, while the other appears as an English-style landscaped garden. Everyone strolling in the park comes

across numerous structures. These are the Temple of Friendship, the Aviary, the Temple of the Three Graces, as well as the monumental mausoleum devoted to Paul I, with the inscription: "To the Consort and Benefactor from Maria Fiodorovna". The architect Thomas de Thomon erected the mausoleum for Maria after Paul I's death, between 1805 and 1810.

Pavlovsk became the Dowager Em-press's favourite place of living. She took care of the palace and park and cultivat-ed flowers there. The Pavlovsk roses were especially famous. They grew near the walls of the elegant Pink Pavilion rebuilt in 1811 at Maria's behest by the architect Andrei Voronikhin from the dacha of the military commandant of Pavlovsk Piotr Bagration into a superb musical salon. The construction work at Pavlovsk ended in 1828 when Maria Fiodorovna had died. The park was her children's favourite place of rest and when Grand Duchess Anna Pavlovna married the heir to the Dutch throne, she redesigned her pal-ace and park at Sustdeik in the style of Pavlovsk – so dear to her were Pavlovsk landscapes and the interiors of her par-ents' palace.

A.G. Rockstuhl. *Portrait of Empress Maria Fiodorovna*. 1866. SM "Peterhof"

Army commander Alexander Suvorov
(1730–1800)

Admiral Fiodor Ushakov (1744–1817)

The foreign policy of Paul I was marked by the same extravagancy as his measures in interior affairs. On concluding a treaty with England as well as with Turkey that had been formerly hostile to Russia, Paul actively engaged in the war against France. Alexander Suvorov, urgently summoned from exile in 1799, at the Sovereign's will marched to North Italy where his troops won victories over the French army in the battles of Adda, Trebbia and Novi, but soon, finding himself practically encircled, had to retreat hastily across the Alps. For the Italian campaign Suvorov was promoted to the rank of Generalissimo and was granted the title of the Prince of Italy. At the same time the Russian naval squadron led by Fiodor Ushakov won several victories in the Mediterranean driving the French from the islands of the Ionic Archipelago, where a republic – the first Greek state independent from the Turks – emerged under the protectorate of Russia. After that Paul suddenly broke Russia's union with England, put a prohibition at English trade and began to draw closer to Napoleon Bonaparte. In 1801 Paul I, in a fantastic move, sent 40 Cossack regiments to conquer British India. The detachment nearly perished in this adventurous campaign that was promptly stopped by Alexander I after his succession.

A. Popov. *Suvorov's Army Crossing the Alps*. 1904

F. Alexeyev. *View of the Mikhailovsky Castle and Connetable Square.* 1800

At the end of his life Paul I built a new residence for himself – the Mikhailovsky Castle (1797–1801). The Emperor wanted to implement in stone his views on architecture based on Romantic notions about knights' castles and, moreover, to create something unlike Catherine's "dissipated" palaces. But Paul was destined to live in his new castle only for about a month. Despite all his good intentions – the establishment of order and justice, the persecution of theft, etc. – his austere, crude rule with sudden wild escapades and unmotivated decisions was generally regarded as unusually despotic and unjustly cruel. Fear and dismay seized society. As for Paul, he lost a sense of reality and lapsed into extremes; he became maniacally suspicious and removed all truly faithful people from himself. All this eventually provoked a group of dissatisfied persons among the Guards and high society to make a conspiracy. The conspiracy ended in bloodshed – the Emperor was killed during the night of 12 March 1801. Thanks to a treason the conspirators penetrated into the thoroughly guarded Mikhailovsky Castle, ascended to the Emperor's bedroom, penetrated there by deceit and killed Paul I in a brawl. Despite the tragic character of this event, society breathed freely. It happened precisely what Paul himself wrote about in his youth denouncing absolute power: "Despotism, engulfing everything, eventually destroys the despot himself."

ALEXANDER I

Alexander Pavlovich,
(12 December 1777, St Petersburg – 19 November 1825, Taganrog),
the Emperor from 11 March 1801

After the murder of Paul I his elder son Alexander ascended to the throne. He was unanimously and enthusiastically greeted in society – young, clever and well educated, the new Emperor gave hopes to become a humane and liberal ruler. Alexander's tutor was the Swiss Republican Frédéric-César de La Harpe to whom Alexander, as he told, owed everything except for his birth. Alexander's liberalism revealed itself at once. In 1801 around the Emperor there formed the so-called Unofficial Committee including the friends of his youth: Pavel Stroganov, Victor Kochubei, Adam Czartoryski and Nikolai Novosiltsov. At the sessions of the committee they discussed plans of turning Russia into a constitutional monarchy and some of these plans to reform the state even began to be implemented. However, Alexander could not ignore a growing resistance to his reforms on the side of the imperial family, the court and the nobility. Finally, quite reasonable fear that dignitaries will use the weakening of the supreme power – and by no means for people's benefit – crept into Alexander's soul. All that cooled the Emperor's reformative zeal. And a struggle against Napoleon that dragged on for many years made the carrying out of the reforms even more difficult.

G. Dawe. *Portrait of Emperor Alexander I.* 1820s.
SM "Peterhof"

G. Schmid from the original by G. Kugelchen.
Emperor Alexander I.
1802–10. SM "Peterhof"

Countess Maria Naryshkina,
lover of Alexander I

Alexander I was a complex and contradictory person. He was inclined to posing and self-conceit; many people thought him to be rancorous, false and insincere, while he was kind and sentimental. Members of the royal family liked him and called him "our angel". Sometime the Emperor could be "weak and sly", to use the words of the poet Alexander Pushkin, but none – neither liberals nor conservatives – succeeded in subordinating him to himself, in breaking his willpower. He evaded direct conflicts, but invariably attained his goal. Perhaps for that reason he was thought to be a skilful diplomat – it is not a mere coincidence that in Napoleon's opinion Alexander as a politician outwitted him.

In 1793, at the age of sixteen, Alexander's grandmother Catherine the Great married him to the fourteen-year-old Luise Marie Auguste, the Margravine of Baden, who took the name of Yelizaveta Alexeyevna on conversion to Orthodoxy. She was a pretty, clever girl with a lofty soul and kind heart. At first the consorts – the charming young couple adored in society – lived fairly well, but after Alexander became the Tsar Elizabeth lost all her influence on him. Their children – Maria and Yelizaveta – died in infancy. Alexander for many years almost openly lived together with his lover, Maria Naryshkina, in her palace at the Fontanka River, while Empress Elizabeth was neglected. Only in 1822 Alexander returned to his wife and they began to live in concord as in their youth. In those years Alexander revealed the most touching care and attention to Elizabeth. It was for the sake of her cure that he went to Taganrog in the autumn of 1825, where he met his death. Elizabeth outlived her husband for a short while and died on 4 May 1826 on the way from Taganrog to Moscow.

J.-L. Mosnier. *Portrait of Empress Yelizaveta Alexeyevna*. 1802. SM "Peterhof"

Wife of Alexander, Princess Louise Marie Auguste of Baden, from 1793 Yelizaveta Alexeyevna (1779–1826)

Despite all his doubts and wavering, however, the reforms continued until 1812 thanks to the efforts of Mikhail Speransky, a major lawyer of the period, who tried to transform the system of government. He supposed to convert autocratic Russia into a constitutional monarchy with a parliament. The clear-cut division of legislative, executive and judicial power was combined in his plans with a provision of franchise to the gentry and merchants. In 1810 Speransky began to create the State Council. Alexander I was, however, not resolute enough to undertake radical reforms and exiled Speransky into a province without any explanation. The lawyer returned to St Petersburg only under Nicholas I.

In the reign of Alexander I the Russian Empire made her first steps into the Caucasus – Georgia joined it. "Under the shelter of friendly bayonets" the Georgians found salvation from their enemies – the Persians, but the annexation of Georgia led to the outbreak of the Caucasian War and Russia's conflicts with the freedom-loving mountaineers of the Northern Caucasus, as roads to Tiflis, the capital of Georgia, passed through their lands.

B. Paterssen. *St Petersburg. Petrovskaya Square.* 1806

Emperor Alexander I

Mikhail Speransky (1772–1839)

Speransky, son of a village priest, studied at a seminary and early revealed his talents. So when he began to work in the Holy Senate in 1797, he made a career as a talented clerk. In 1808 he became Deputy Minister of the Interior and the Tsar brought his nearer to himself. In 1810 Speransky was made the Secretary of State and one of Alexander's closest associates. Thanks to his outstanding abilities of an analytic, systematist and reformer, as well as vast knowledge of the state structure of Russia and other countries, Speransky became the Tsar's principal adviser on reforms.

In 1810 Speransky began to realize a plan for the creation of the State Council and a system of ministries, but Alexander suspected him of scheming and exiled him to the province. Later, in 1818–21, Speransky became the Governor-General of Siberia, but he could return to St Petersburg only in the reign of Nicholas I. There were several reasons for Speransky's exile and curtailing of reforms: against them were the Tsar's entire entourage, his mother, high society and the gentry. The former tutor of the Emperor La Harpe also came out against the reforms. He wrote to his pupil from abroad that "once the project of the Senate is accepted, the monarch merely retains his name." The Swiss knew Russian society very well and he had no illusions about the intentions of senators and the Russian nobility: "Don't allow to mislead you owing to a disgust you have to the unlimited power. Have a courage to preserve it entirely until the moment when the necessary works will be completed under your supervision, and you will be able to leave as much power for you as is necessary for an energetic government'" And the last thing was that Alexander was offended by Speransky's suggestion to summon a parliament – the Council – and entrust to it the waging of war against Napoleon. After that he fell in disgrace.

Ink set of Alexander I. Russia, St Petersburg. Made by A. Gedlund. 1800–10. SM "Peterhof"

Frederick, King of Prussia, and Alexander I swearing to keep eternal friendship at the burial place of Frederick the Great

At first Russia's relations with Napoleon were quite peaceful, but in 1802–03 Emperor Alexander largely changed his position – he could not suppress his irritation at seeing the success of the first consul of France. In fact, Russia had no strategic interests in her struggle started together with Austria against the "usurper", but the allies were eager to "teach the impudent" who dared to declare himself the Emperor in 1804! Alexander stroke up a great friendship with King Frederick William III of Prussia, but all noticed that the Tsar was more enamoured of his consort, Queen Louise. In November 1805 the three of them descended to the burial vault of Frederick II and swore friendship on the tomb of the great military leader.

The first wars against Napoleon ended in 1805 by the defeat of the Russian troops near Austerlitz. The Tsar himself, unsuccessful in action, ran away from the battlefield and ever since abstained

P. Oduen, J. Duplessis-Bertaux and Bovinet from the original by Ch. Chatillon.
Napoleon. The Battle of Austerlitz. 1805. Detail. SM "Peterhof"

from participation in combat realizing that warfare was not for him. In 1806 the war against Napoleon resumed and on 26–27 January 1807 the Russians and Prussians, their allies, succeeded to repel the onslaught of the French army at Preussisch-Eulau near Königsberg with terrible losses, but later Napoleon defeated the Russians at Friedland. After that Alexander had to seek for peace with Napoleon Bonaparte. On 25 June 1807, near the town of Tilsit, Alexander embraced on a raft in the middle of the Niemen the man whom he had recently christened the "enemy of mankind". After their talks on the raft Russia concluded an alliance treaty with France and broke relations with England, Napoleon's enemy. However, nobody doubted that the Treaty of Tilsit was fragile and a new war was inevitable.

F. Chevalier. *Napoleon I Bonaparte*. 1838. SM "Peterhof"

Alexander I meeting Napoleon on the Niemen River in June 1807

Army commander, General-Field Marshal
Mikhail Barclay de Tolly (1761–1818)

The war that began in 1812 threatened for a long time. Russia's union with France was unstable and Napoleon's appetites were growing – he dreamed of world domination. Over the years his irritation with regard to Russia was accumulating. He was hurt by Alexander's unwillingness to give his sister, Grand Duchess Yekaterina Pavlovna, in marriage to him. Alexander himself also suffered greatly from his defeats and forced friendship with Napoleon. The Tsar greatly changed in those years. His former illusions dispelled like clouds, his Romanticism disappeared and it was difficult to bear the burden of ruling the large country on his shoulders. When Napoleon started his invasion of Russia in the summer of 1812, the Russian army began to retreat to the hinterland. Alexander I entrusted the command to Mikhail Barclay de Tolly and left the troops bearing in mind his unsuccessful participation in the battle of Austerlitz. The army was retreating

Unknown artist. *Fire at Smolensk on 16–18 August 1812*. 1816

with battles and this led to the growth of discontent in society. Alexander decided to meet public opinion and appointed Mikhail Kutuzov as the Commander-in-Chief, although he did not like him. On his return from the Emperor Kutuzov uttered a joke: "Probably I won't be able to win, but I'll try to outwit the enemy." But he still did not manage to evade a large-scale battle. It took place near the village of Borodino, some seventy-five miles from Moscow, on 26 August 1812. After the first day of the bloody battle, having evaluated the terrific losses, Kutuzov made up his mind to disengage and to withdraw farther and surrendered Moscow to the French army. Despite the loss of the old capital, Alexander was steadfast and would not

Mikhail Golenishchev-Kutuzov,
the Most Illustrious Prince of Smolensk
(1745–1813)

I. M. Guérin. *Piotr Bagration Wounded in the Battle of Borodino.* 1816

Emperor Alexander I, Grand Duke Konstantin Pavlovich and Count Mikhail Barclay de Tolly with the General Staff marching at the Champs d'Elysées in Paris on 19 March 1814

View of the Triumphal Gate erected in honour of the Russian Imperial Guards and the majestic procession in St Petersburg on 31 July 1814

engage in any negotiations with Napoleon after a great conflagration and devastation of Moscow the invader had to retreat. In December 1812 Alexander I gladdened Russia by his manifesto about the complete expulsion of Napoleon. The Russian Emperor, thrilled by the victory, demanded, despite Kutuzov's opinion, to persecute Napoleon's army beyond the borders of Russia for the ultimate defeat of his empire. In January 1813 the Russian army led by Kutuzov crossed the Niemen and its foreign campaign began. In the spring of 1814 the Russian troops invaded France and Alexander I entered Paris on the white horse once presented to him by Napoleon. The enemy was defeated.

The victory over Napoleon united the major states of Europe as nothing else. They took a decision to establish a new European order. Essentially, though, this order was an old one, i.e. it restored in Europe the former, pre-revolutionary borders and regimes, which had largely become obsolete by 1814. At the Vienna Congress of 1814 Russia, Austria, Prussia and other countries concluded the Holy Alliance for struggle against any revolutionary attempts. Alexander I then grew concerned with the creation of the new world order with the Holy Alliance and Russia at the head. No interior reforms were mentioned any more.

Emperor Alexander I

I. Ivanov. *Celebration in St Petersburg on 19 March 1816 in Honour of the Entry of the Russian and Allied Armies into Paris*. 1816

Statesman and military
figure Alexei Arakcheyev
(1769–1834)

Alexander regarded
Arakcheyev as a reliable and
faithful man and that was
really so. Arakcheyev wrote:
"I was guided in my life by
rules alone – I never reasoned
in my service and fulfilled
all orders literally devoting
all my time and efforts to
the royal service. I know that
many people do not like me
because I am severe, but what
is to be done? God created me
like this! I was also severely
turned around, and I've
remained thankful for that.
You cannot forge an action by
sweet French talking!"

In that period General Alexei Arakcheyev, a man
wholeheartedly faithful to the Tsar, but conservative and
narrow-minded, moved to the foreground of political life
in the state. Encouraged by Alexander, he paid especial
attention to the creation of the so-called "military settlements", which would allow to reduce drastically the cost
of the army. Around 1818 rumours and denunciations
about the activities of some clandestine societies reached
the authorities. This information worried Alexander I and
his entourage. The authorities regarded with particular
suspicion masonic lodges with their mystic symbolism. In
1822 the austere decree was issued prohibiting any secret

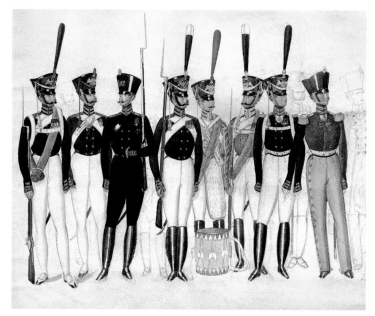

Unknown artist. Samples of military uniform from the reign of Emperor Alexander I.
First decades of the 19th century. SM "Peterhof"

societies including masonic lodges in Russia. This measure,
however, did not stop either masons or revolutionaries.

As is known, Emperor Paul I and Maria Fiodorovna
had many children. After the death of his father, Alexander
found himself to be at the head of a large family consisting
of his wife, mother, three brothers and five sisters, whose
weddings he was supposed to arrange. But as regards
family affairs, he did not make a single step without an
advice of his mother, the Dowager Empress Maria Fiodorovna. Some historians believe that during the night
of her husband's murder, 11 March 1801, she heard the

noise of a struggle and not just knocked at the closed door of her husband's bedroom (he had lived separately from her for a long time), but allegedly tried to seize power and to become the second Catherine the Great. The Dowager Empress devoted the period of her widowhood mostly to charity. The Charitable Society she created later bore her name and became a symbol of mercy and love for one's neighbour. In spite of her age, Maria Fiodorovna continued to lead a very active life. Strong, fresh and still retaining beauty, she was never ill and never knew tiredness, tears or depression. With German pedantry, accuracy and rigour she made her good social deeds as earlier had carried on the management of Paul's family. Empress Maria died in October 1828 surprised by an unknown mortal disease. To the very end she did not believe that she was dying.

МАТЬ РОССІИ

Что смерть?.... Безсмертная Она,
Великихъ Мать, Великая жена.

Ye. Skotnikov. *Empress Maria Fiodorovna*. 1828.
SM "Peterhof"

A. Novikov from the original by P. Svinyin. *View of the Great Cascade with an Illumination on the Saint's Day of Empress Maria Fiodorovna*. 1818. SM "Peterhof"

G. Kügelchen. *The Family of Emperor Paul I.* 1800

Different fates befell the sisters of Alexander I. After an abortive attempt to give the elder daughter, Alexandra Pavlovna, in marriage to Gustav IV of Sweden, Paul gave his consent in 1799 for her marriage to the Austrian Prince Josef. In March 1801 Alexandra died in childbirth at the age of eighteen. The life of her sister, Yelena Pavlovna, married to Frederick, Prince of Mecklenburg, was quite happy with him, but also broke suddenly. Her doctors discovered galloping consumption that brought the nineteen-year-old woman to her grave.

The death of the two sisters struck Alexander I and his mother. They thought much before giving in marriage the third sister, Maria Pavlovna – wouldn't this young girl leave them to die soon, too? But there was a happy end in her case. Maria married the Prince of Weimar, later became a duchess and won renown throughout Europe for her fine education, clever mind and love for art. She befriended Schiller, Goethe and Franz Liszt.

Sister of Alexander I, Grand Duchess Alexandra Pavlovna (1783–1801)

Yekaterina Pavlovna, the next sister, also gave a lot of troubles to the royal family. It was to her that Napoleon made a proposal to marriage but was turned down. In 1809 Maria Fiodorovna breathed freely after giving her daughter in marriage to Prince George of Oldenburg. In 1812 Georg died and two years later her new choice became Prince Wilhelm, the successor of Württemberg. Yekaterina had a reputation of a clever and strong-willed woman. Unlike her other brothers and sisters, she enjoyed Alexander's particular trust and exerted a strong, if not always beneficial, influence upon

Sister of Alexander I, Grand Duchess
Yelena Pavlovna (1784–1803)

Sister of Alexander I, Grand Duchess
Maria Pavlovna (1786–1859)

Sister of Alexander I,
Grand Duchess
Yekaterina Pavlovna
(1788–1818)

him. On settling in Stuttgart, the capital of Württemberg, she turned her court into a centre of education and culture. The sudden death of Yekaterina Pavlovna in January 1819 from erysipelas that killed the young woman became a great surprise for everybody.

The last of Paul I's daughters, Anna, also evaded in 1810 a marriage to Napoleon, who did not abandon hope to become related with the Romanov family and after Yekaterina's refusal proposed as husband to the fifteen-year-old Anna. In 1818 she married Prince Wilhelm of the Netherlands, who ascended the throne in 1840. So the present-day royal dynasty in Holland is descended from Queen Anna Pavlovna.

Sister of Emperor Alexander I, Grand Duchess
Anna Pavlovna (1795–1865) with her husband,
the Netherlandish Prince William of Orange

Alexander I died in Taganrog at 11:50 on 19 November 1825. His body was embalmed and brought to St Petersburg. The death of the Emperor, an energetic man of good health, at forty-seven, in some distant corner of Russia, caused rumours that the real Tsar did not die. It was alleged that he disguised himself under the name of the *starets* Fiodor Kuzmich, who won fame by his wisdom, right-eousness and humility as well as, what was remarkable, by his simi-larity to the deceased Emperor Alexander I. The *starets* made a

Starets Fiodor Kuzmich (?–1864)

КОНЧИНА ГОСУДАРЯ ИМПЕРАТОРА АЛЕКСАНДРА ПЕРВАГО въ ТАГАНРОГѢ 19 Ноября 1825.

A. Afanasyev. *The Death of Emperor Alexander I at Taganrog.* 1825. SM "Peterhof"

Unknown engraver. *View of the Mournful Chariot Carrying the Body of the Deceased Emperor Alexander.*
1825. SM "Peterhof"

pilgrimage to the holy places of Russia and then settled in Siberia where he died in 1864. Who was that starets, is a mystery to this day. Weighing all pros and contras, we can only assert that during the last years of his rule Alexander I lost an interest in power and glory and dreamed to abandon the throne. He said about that many times to his entourage.

Contemporaries noticed that during the last year of his life Alexander changed beyond recognition. Some important idea possessed the Tsar making him pensive and decisive at the same time. The idea to leave the throne and mix with the people by taking the guise of a pilgrim was not alien to him. Pilgrims with their long journeys along an endless road and with faith visible in their eyes might prompt an outcome for Alexander, too. Alexandra Fiodorovna, the consort of Nicholas I, made the following entry in her diary on 15 August 1826, a week before their coronation: "Probably at the sight of people I'll think how the deceased Emperor Alexander, while telling us about his abdication, added: 'How glad I'll be to see you passing by me and to cry myself 'Hurrah!' to you in the crowd and swing my fur cap'."

CONSTANTINE I

Konstantin Pavlovich
(27 April 1779, Tsarskoye Selo – 15 June 1831, Vitebsk)
the Emperor from 27 November to 14 December 1825

A point of departure for the dramatic events that occurred in St Petersburg in December 1825 was the news from Taganrog about the death of Alexander I. Earlier, in 1822, he had bequeathed the throne not to the elder of his brothers, Konstantin, but to the younger one, Nikolai. However, nobody besides the most trusted persons knew about that will. Therefore the Senate and the Holy Synod, having received the sad news from Taganrog, proclaimed Tsesarevich Konstantin Pavlovich as Emperor Constantine. This is how the brief reign of Constantine I began. The troops vowed fidelity to him without asking his permission, toasts were proposed to him and coins with profile were minted. And only on 13 December 1825 Constantine's final abdication from the throne arrived. It was only then that Nicholas could occupy the vacant throne in a legal way.

The group of rebellious officers who would later become known as the Decembrists tried to use the interregnum to their own favour. The members of the revolutionary society with a wide network decided to rebel at the moment when the army would give its oath of allegiance to Emperor Nicholas I. The mutiny that began in the morning of 14 December (hence the name of its participants), but soon serious miscalculations of its organizers became evident.

Workshop of G. Dawe. *Portrait of Grand Duke Konstantin Pavlovich*.
1829. SM "Pavlovsk"

F. John from the original by J.-H. Benner. *Portrait of Grand Duke Konstantin Pavlovich*. 1800–20. SM "Peterhof"

Grand Duke Konstantin Pavlovich more than his brothers resembled Paul both in his appearance and hot temper. He was unlucky in his family life with Grand Duchess Anna Fiodorovna (Julie Henriette Ulrike, Princess of Saxe-Saafeld-Coburg), who ran away to her relations in Germany soon after their wedding. That was due to his furious conduct – it was not for nothing that he was nicknamed "a despotic whirlwind". Many years later, in Warsaw, where Tsesarevich Konstantin Pavlovich had been appointed the Successor under Alexander I, the grand duke met Countess Ioanna Grudzinska and passionately fell in love with her. He divorced Anna Fiodorovna, received with difficulty a consent of his mother, the Dowager Empress Maria Fiodorovna, for a new marriage and married his love, who was granted the title of Princess Lowicz from Alexander I. Living in Poland, he came to love its culture and people, yet steadily and cruelly carried out there an imperial policy of the autocracy. When a revolt suddenly began in Poland, he had to flee from the belvedere Palace. The Tsesarevich was nearly out of his mind from sorrow and despair as he felt himself betrayed by the Poles who he so loved. In Vitebsk, where he had to retreat, he got ill with cholera and died in 1831.

W. Sliwizki. *Portrait of Princess Lowicz.* 1827. SM "Peterhof"

The second wife of Grand Duke Konstantin Pavlovich Ioanna Grudzinska, Princess Lowicz (1795–1831)

A. Ivanov from the original by V. Sadovnikov. *View of the Great Palace at Strelna*. 1833

Attack of the Belvedere Palace in 1830

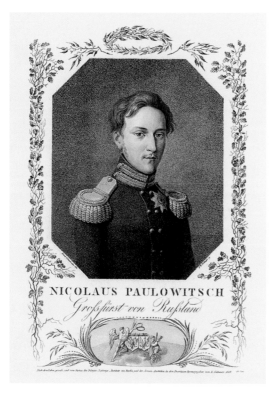

F. V. Bollinger from the original by P. E. Gebauer.
Grand Duke Nikolai Pavlovich. 1818.
SM "Peterhof"

F. John from the original by J.-H. Benner.
Portrait of Grand Duke Konstantin Pavlovich. 1800–20.
SM "Peterhof"

C. Collmann. *Senate Square in St Petersburg. 14 December 1825.* 1830s

They brought the units loyal to them from their barracks to Senate Square too late and did not show the resolution and co-ordination necessary in that moment. Those faithful to Nicholas I also lingered – he still wavered as a young inexperienced man. Towards the evening, as a result of the passive conduct of the rebels, who kept the soldiers loyal to him on the square for no reason, the initiative naturally passed to Nicholas, who suppressed the revolt by gun fire. Later the mutiny of the Chernigov Regiment in the Ukraine was also suppressed. The arrested rebels and conspirators (totally 316) were put into the casemates of the Peter and Paul Fortress. The investigation began there and the special Supreme Criminal Court had its sessions in the fortress.

Nicholas I, who proved to be a good inquirer, supervised all the phases of the investigation himself. The criminals were divided into eleven degrees according to their guilt. The five leaders were hung at the *kronwerk* of the Peter and Paul Fortress and the rest were exiled to Siberia. Investigations and trials of the participants in the revolt still continued for a long time in other cities and towns. The Decembrists' revolt led to very grave consequences to the whole country. The outstanding people perished or were exiled and social life became frozen by fear and despondency. As for the authorities, after the terrible shock of the rebellious days they began to regard any suggestions connected with modernization and necessary changes in the country with great mistrust.

The Constantine coin.
Copy of the 19th century.
SM "Peterhof"

NICHOLAS I

Nikolai Pavlovich
(25 June 796, Tsarskoye Selo – 18 February 1855, St Petersburg),
the Emperor from 14 December 1825

The twenty-nine-year-old Nicholas I, who ascended the throne in the terrific situation of a revolt, was at first diffident and doubtful. He sincerely wished good for Russia, but being not prepared to the role of the autocrat, he did not receive good education, did not like books and did not possess the wide range of interests necessary for a statesman. Nicholas early became infatuated with square-bashing, marching and manual of the rifle, in which he saw the sense of military training. A mighty and beautiful warrior, he still would never become either a great military reformer or a great army leader. Manoeuvres near Krasnoye Selo or a parade on the Field of Mars were for him the consummation of the military commander's art. Naturally, the new Emperor understood that Russia needed reforms, but did not possess the political will and resolution of a reformer. He was especially afraid to damage the invariable foundations sacred to him – autocracy, empire, serfdom and the landlords' possession of the land. His reign turned out to be the age of stagnation and reaction that left with his contemporaries only the feelings of regret for the lost possibilities. Nicholas was happy in his family life. In 1817 he married Alexandra Fiodorovna (Friederike Luise Charlotte Wilhelmine), the daughter of the Prussian King Frederick

G. Dawe. *Portrait of Grand Duke Nikolai Pavlovich*. 1820s.
SM "Peterhof"

C. Schultz after a drawing by Ye. Meyer. *The Cottage Palace in the Alexandria Park*. Mid-19th century. SM "Peterhof"

Case of drawing instruments of Nicholas I. Russia, St Petersburg. Made by A. Samoilov. The Izhora Admiralty Works. 1830s. SM "Peterhof"

Casket with flasks, belonged to Nicholas I. France (?). Early 19th century. SM "Peterhof"

Emperor Nicholas I with his favourite dog Hussar

William III. The young people liked each other at the first glance. Alexandra Fiodorovna seemed to be a woman of unearthly beauty and elegance to many people. They wrote that she resembled a careless exotic bird seated in a golden cage, while her consort, Nicholas, was treating her to some heavenly refreshments. Alexandra had a beautiful character, she was kind, not rancorous and good-natured. At the same time she was unbiased, never refused to help anybody and engaged in charity with pleasure. She was patient and faithful. On learning about an intension of the Decembrists' wives to follow their exiled husbands to Siberia, she exclaimed: "I would do the same in their place!" On the days of her husband's succession she said: "My lot is still fine. I'll be his friend on the throne, too! And that is all for me!" The Empress invariably was the first beauty – nobody in Russia danced or dressed oneself better than she. Alexander named their suburban residence at Peterhof, where the architect Adam Menelaws built for the imperial family a small and cosy suburban house in the "Gothic" style, the Cottage, in honour of his consort – Alexandria. Infatuated with the Neo-Gothic fashion, the Emperor seemed to have built a special world for himself, for his soul, in secret, as it were, from the sumptuous Empire-style capi-tal – he wanted to live not in a gilded palatial space, visible from all sides, but on his "estate", and Alexandria met this demand. The talented architect Andrei

Rose in a Pot.
Jeweller
J.G. Hossauer.
Berlin, Germany.
1852.
SM "Peterhof"

Hossauer's present to Empress Alexandra Fiodorovna for her birthday.

Wife of Nicholas I
Friederike Louise Charlotte
Wilhelmine, Princess
of Prussia, from 1817
Alexandera Fiodorovna
(1798–1860)

A. Briullov. *Portrait of Empress Alexandra Fiodorovna in the Drawing Room of the Cottage.* 1830. SM "Peterhof"

Chatelaine with a set of objects for handwork (scissors, needle-case, finger-tip and hook) bequeathed by Empress Maria Fiodorovna to her daughter-in-law Alexandra Fiodorovna. France (?). Early 19th century. SM "Peterhof"

The Potsdam Cup. Made by J.G. Hossauer. Berlin, Germany. 1830. SM "Peterhof"

The silver cup is adorned with enamel coats of arms of the participants of the "Magic of White Rose" festival that was held in 1829 in Potsdam in honour of Alexandra Fiodorovna.

Tournament book of Empress Alexandra Fiodorovna. 13 July 1829. The book has fifty pages and each of them bears a drawn shield with the mottoes of the knights, participants in the Magic of White Rose festival. SM "Peterhof"

Award tokens of the Order of the Rose. Jeweller J.G. Hossauer, from a sketch by Empress Alexandra Fiodorovna. Berlin, Germany. 1829. SM "Peterhof"

Th. Wright from the original by G. Dawe. *Empress Alexandra Fiodorovna with Grand Duchess Maria Nikolayevna and Grand Duke Alexander Nikolayevich*. 1825. SM "Peterhof"

Unknown engraver. *Portrait of Grand Duchess Maria Nikolayevna and Duke Maximilian of Leuchtenberg.* 1840. SM "Peterhof"

Ring with a portrait of Emperor Nicholas I. St Petersburg, Russia. 1837.
SM "Peterhof"

It belonged to Grand Duchess Maria Nikolayevna, daughter of Nicholas I

Stackenschneider decorated St Petersburg and Peterhof with magnificent palaces and diverse pavilions – the Tsarina's Pavilion was put up for Alexandra Fiodorovna and Olga's Pavilion was erected for Nicholas' daughter, Olga.

Among the Emperor's seven children historians usually singled out his first child Grand Duke Alexander (the future Emperor Alexander II), Grand Duchess Olga Nikolayevna, later the Queen of Württemberg, as well as Grand Duchess Alexandra Nikolayevna, a young girl of rare beauty and a talented singer, who died of consumption several months after her wedding with Frederick William, the heir to the Danish throne. The youngest son of Nicholas I, Grand Duke and General-Admiral Konstantin Nikolayevich, who showed himself during the age of the Great Reforms, also was an outstanding man.

Items from the service of the dowry of Emperor Nicholas I's daughter, Grand Duchess Olga Nikolayevna. Imperial Porcelain Works, St Petersburg, Russia. 1846. SM "Peterhof"

C. Schultz from a drawing by Ye. Meyer.
View of Tsaritsyn Island. Mid-19th century.
SM "Peterhof"

Daughter of
Nicholas I
Grand Princess
Olga Nikolayevna
(1822–1892)

Daughter of
Nicholas I
Grand Princess
Alexandra
Nikolayevna
(1825–1844)

Schmid from the original by G. Schwarz. *The Entry of Emperor Nicholas I to Krasnoye Selo*. 1849–52. SM "Peterhof"

Russia's leadership in Europe after 1814 was generally admitted, but it was not so in the East. Russia's neighbours in the Caucasus, Persia and Turkey, did not like her policy in the region very much. In 1826 the immense Persian army of Abbas Mirza declared war on Russia, but the Russian troops rather easily defeated the Persians in several battles. On 10 February 1828 a treaty was signed in the village of Turkmanchai that gave Russia the eastern part of Armenia with the city of Erivan. Meanwhile a new conflict ripened in the south of the country. Russia engaged in the war of England and France against Turkey that was responsible for a bloody massacre in Greece. The naval battle of Navarino of 1827 became a prologue for the Russo-Turkish War on land. This war that broke out in 1828 proved to be rather successful for Russia. The Russian army crossed the Danube, forced several Turkish fortresses to surrender and reached the outskirts of Stambul, but Nicholas didn't give orders to capture the capital of Turkey, as that would lead to numerous international complications.

НИКОЛАЙ I.   NICOLAUS I.

F. Jentzen from the original by F. von Krüger. *Emperor Nicholas I with His Suite*. 1831–40. SM "Peterhof"

Unknown artist. *Portrait of General Alexei Yermolov* (1772–1861). 1861. SM "Peterhof"

The efforts of the Russian army in the Caucasus were successful – the Turkish fortresses Kars and Erzerum fell under its pressure. The two parties signed the Treaty of Adrianople in September 1829. That settlement gave Russia the mouth of the Danube and the Black Sea coast from Anapa to Poti, including the shore of Abkhazia, became the property of Russia. Moldavia and Serbia gained autonomy within the Ottoman Empire and Greece enjoyed greater independence.

The mutiny of the Polish army in Warsaw came as a great shock for Nicholas I in November 1830. The Tsar was especially indignant of the "ingratitude" of the Poles who had more privileges than his other subjects and nevertheless "dared" to officially declare the overthrow of Nicholas I from the Polish throne at the session of the Polish Sejm on 13 January 1831. But it is known that the revolt began because the Russian authorities violated the constitution

Unknown artist. *The taking of Erzerum*. First decades of the 19th century

A. Charlemagne. Everyday, usual and festive uniforms of court cavaliers.
1855. SM "Peterhof"

granted to the Poles in 1815. The bloody battles of Grochow and Ostrolenka ended with the victories of the Russian troops and in August Warsaw fell under their pressure. The war soon ended. Many Poles fled to the West, the captured rebels were executed or exiled to Siberia.

With the foundation of the fortress Groznaya (the future town of Grozny) on the Sunzha River in 1818 and the advance of the Russian troops into the mountains the Caucasian War began. The brutal policy of General Alexei Yermolov, the Russian Governor of the Caucasus, led to the growth of the mountaineers' resistance. The religious movement of Muridism began to grow among them, which united most of the formerly disintegrated tribes in their fight against the punitive expeditions. General Ivan Paskevich, Yermolov's successor, tried to establish Russia's dominance over the entire Black Sea coast of the Caucasus, which led to the formation of the new front of struggle against the mountaineers. The 1840s and 1850s were spent fighting against Shamil's imamate that was defeated only in the early 1860s.

General-Field Marshal
Ivan Paskevich
(1782–1856)

Having now an outlet to the Black Sea and advancing far along its eastern and western coasts, Russia wanted one thing more – to conquer Constantinople and the straits. The obvious weakening of Turkey favoured these intentions. But the "keys to the East" lying at the Bosporus were no less attractive for other states – England and France. It was with them that Russia failed to divide their zones of influence at the Near East. Pushing back the Turks, Nicholas I supposed that England and France rivalling each other would not be able to unite and support the Osmans, but he made an error in his counting. Starting the war on Turkey Russia son had to face the English-French coalition.

Emperor Nicholas I

Unknown artist. *The Arch of the Main Staff Building*. Second quarter of the 19th century. SM "Peterhof"

At first no great problems could be envisaged in this war for Russia. In 1853 the squadron led by Pavel Nakhimov destroyed a Turkish squadron in the Sinop Bay. But before long the English-French squadron entered the Black Sea and the Russian Fleet found itself blocked up in the Sevastopol Bay. In September 1854 the allies landed in the Crimea, defeated the Russian army on the Alma River and besieged Sevastopol. Despite the heroic defence that lasted for 349 days in September 1855 the fortress had to surrender. The ambitious Nicholas I was unable to bear the shame of an impending defeat. Legend has it that on seeing through a spyglass the flags of the English-French squadron blocking the Kronstadt, the Tsar made up his mind to settle all his accounts in this world and drunk poison in the Winter Palace on 18 February 1855.

A. Beggrow from the original by A. Teichel. The hall on the ground floor of the Winter Palace, where the body of Emperor Nicholas was put for leave-taking. 1855. SM "Peterhof"

ALEXANDER II

Alexander II Nikolayevich
(17 April 1818, Moscow – 1 March 1881, St Petersburg)
the Emperor from 18 February 1855

One of the tutors of the new Tsar was the poet Vasily Zhukovsky, who allegedly at once said to Alexander's parents that he would prepare not a regiment commander but an enlightened monarch, who must regard Russia as a nation rather than as drilling grounds or barracks. In general, the eventual result corresponded to the intention. Alexander II received a good education and for a long time seriously prepared himself to the accession. So he knew well the real state of affairs in the country and the moods of people. He often visited foreign countries having an opportunity to compare the Russian way of life with foreign living standards. Many of the things introduced in his reign in Russia did not satisfy the Emperor, but he understood the vital importance of transformations for the strengthening of the state and the regime.

Alexander was smart and tall. Light and agile, he was known as a fine rider, brave and composed man. These qualities revealed themselves during incessant attempts of revolutionaries upon his life. The accession of Alexander II to the throne inspired many people, although society did not immediately accept the idea of radical transformations. Many adherents of reforms did not go, even in their dreams, as far the government would later dare to advance.

Ye. Botman. Portrait of Emperor Alexander II.
1875. The Russian Museum

But society gradually began to share liberal ideas, and the change in views owed much to Alexander Herzen who published in London the almanac *The Polar Star* and the newspaper *The Bell*, forbidden but unusually popular in Russia. They were read everywhere, a stream of letters came to Herzen from Russia, and he published them, too. The years between 1856 and 1861 were the period of "glasnost". It was Herzen who appealed to the Tsar: "Our Sovereign, give freedom to the Russian word. Our minds are tightened, our thoughts poison our breast due to the lack of expanse and it moans in censure stocks… Give us a free speech… We have what to say to the world and to our people…" And soon, to the horror of the conservatives, one could read in the press the things for which one would be driven to the police in the reign of Nicholas I. And suddenly the age of Nicholas fell back as a tombstone over the living people – the censure became less strict, the military settlements were abolished, prohibitions were cancelled one after another and they began to give foreign passports! In the situation of general disarray, heated debates about the ways, means and tempo of reforms a public opinion was being formed. It sided with the young Emperor, who was called the "Tsar Liberator" not by court flatterers alone, but by the popular masses as well.

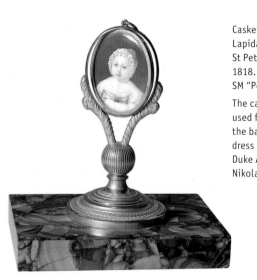

I. Vinberg.
Portrait of Grand Duke Alexander Nikolayevich.
After 1836.
SM "Peterhof"

Casket. Peterhof Lapidary Works, St Petersburg. 1818.
SM "Peterhof"

The casket was used for keeping the baptismal dress of Grand Duke Alexander Nikolayevich.

Paper-weight with a portrait of Grand Duke Alexander Nikolayevich in a baptismal shirt. St Petersburg, Russia. 1818–19. SM "Peterhof"

The Anointing of Emperor Alexander II. From the *Coronation Book of Alexander II*. 1856

Emperor Alexander II

Pocket watch
of Alexander II.
London,
England. 1867.
SM "Peterhof"

The Emperor
had this watch
the day of his
tragic death.

Table wallet with a mirrored
initial of Alexander II.
Paris, France.
SM "Peterhof"

Brother of
Alexander II Grand
Duke Konstantin
Nikolayevich
(1827–1892)

The programme of reforms was ripening in the depth of power for a long time. The Tsar happened to have good associates and assistants in his activities aimed at the transformation of the country. These were the Tsar's brother, Grand Duke Konstantin Nikolayevich, Yakov Rostovtsev, Nikolai and Dmitry Miliutin, Piotr Valuyev and others. The conservatives disliked the younger brother of Alexander II, Grand Duke Konstantin, more than others. They believed that it was he who incited the Emperor to "ruin Russia" inspiring him to enact reforms. A well-

Carved pen in the shape
of a feather, belonged
to Alexander II.
West Europe.
SM "Peterhof"

educated and clever man, a connoisseur of music and painting, Konstantin was an outstanding naval minister, a General-Admiral who began the reconstruction of the Russian Fleet, the Chairman of the State Council and primarily an outstanding statesman of a liberal trend.

The central event of the age of reforms was the abolition of serfdom on 19 February 1861. This measure was of great importance to an immense part of the population and caused other reforms in the fields of management, court, army, finance and education. In 1864 the *zemstvos* – organs of local self-government responsible for local economic problems and hospitals and schools in the countryside – were established for the first time in Russia. The essential things in the court reform were an introduction of the jury, a competitive principle for the parties as well as a right for one's defence and for an independent barrister.

It was difficult to govern the foreign policy of the defeated country – the Treaty of Paris concluded after the Crimean War in 1856 humiliated Russia by depriving it of the fleet in the Black Sea. It was necessary to radically revise Russia's foreign policy. Alexander Gorchakov, the new Minister of Foreign Affairs, informed all the states by his first official instruction that Russia cancelled all

Statesman, Senator Nikolai Miliutin (1818–1872)

War Minister Dmitry Miliutin (1816–1912)

Alexander II reading the Manifesto about the abolishment of serfdom

its moral obligations to the members of the Sacred Union and was going to concentrate on "the development of the country's inner resources". The Caucasian War was at last completed in 1859 – Shamil surrendered to the mercy of the victors.

The war against Turkey started in 1877, despite all optimistic expectations of generals and Alexander II, who arrived himself in the army, proved to be fierce and bloody. At first the army sent to the Balkans under the banner of the liberation of the Slavs, who rebelled against the Turks, forced the Danube and rapidly pushed forward. The Romanians and Bulgars met the army with flowers. Knocking

Minister of Foreign Affairs
Prince Alexander Gorchakov (1798–1883)

The capture
of Ardagan
and of Kars

Alexander II on a march

Alexander II thanking General Gurko after the capture of Telish

the Turks out of the Shipka Gorge, the Russian regiments opened for themselves a way to Stambul. However, soon the Turks' resistance increased and with the approach of the winter the army began to suffer immense losses. Only in December 1877 the army commanded by Iosif Gurko started from the recently taken Plevna, crossed the Balkans by icebound mountainous roads and occupied Sophia. In January 1878 the army of Mikhail Skobelev reached the village of San Stefano some miles from Istanbul and talks began. According to the treaty the Balkan countries became independent from the Osman Empire, although the gains were somewhat curtailed at the Berlin Congress of 1878.

In 1878 a decisive turn towards the introduction of the constitutional government began in Russia. The idea of the constitution was discussed both in the government and society. All that took place in the situation of terror unleashed by the People's Will against the Emperor. In 1880–81 the government was headed by Mikhail Loris-Melikov, a combat general, experienced administrator and an adroit politician. He was supposed to push the reforms forward and at the same time to suppress the terror. Loris-Melikov convinced the Tsar to begin a discussion of the constitutional projects without delay. After considering Loris-Melikov's projects Alexander II told on 1 March 1881 that he had made "the first step to the constitution".

I. Kramskoi. *Portrait of Emperor Alexander II.* 1860–70. SM "Peterhof"

Count Mikhail Loris-Melikov (1825–1888)

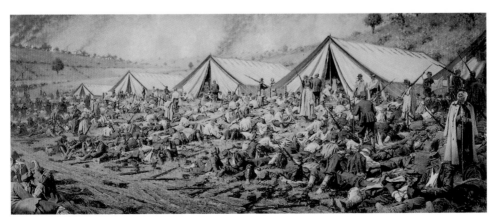

V. Vereschagin. After the Attack at Plevna. 1881

Profile portrait of Alexander II.
Workshop of C. Saolini.
Italy. 1860s.
SM "Peterhof"

On the same day he was killed by the terrorists on the Catherine Canal Embankment. The first bomb thrown by Nicholas Rysakov destroyed the carriage of the Emperor, the second bomb cut Alexander's life short. When smoke dispersed after the explosion, the witnesses saw a terrific picture: about twenty people were wounded or killed, "amidst snow, garbage and blood the remains of torn clothes, shoulder straps, swords and the bloody lumps of man's meat could be seen." Alexander III had his legs broken off. The bleeding Emperor was put on sledges and brought to the Winter Palace where he soon died.

The attempts of the Free Will terrorists at the life of the Tsar began more frequent in 1879, but they failed and the Tsar revealed

After the first explosion Alexander II went out of his carriage and then Grinevitsky threw the second bomb.

Cross. West Europe. Second half of the 19th century. SM "Peterhof"

It belonged to Alexander II, brought from Jerusalem.

Carriage pillow.
Russia. 1870s.
SM "Peterhof"

The pillow was in Alexander II's carriage on the day when the Emperor was mortally wounded.

personal bravery not changing his habits to have walks and in general continued to feel himself the master in his country. Eventually the terrorists used this factor. They were dangerous fanatics and did not care to save not only their own their lives, but also the lives of those innocent people who died during their attempts at the Tsar. Meanwhile the police steadily followed their tracks and arrested Andrei Zheliabov, the leader of the People's Will. However, the group of "bombers" led by Zheliabov's assistant and lover, Sophia Perovskaya, completed their evil deed.

The chapel erected on the Catherine Canal in memory of the death of Emperor Alexander II

The Catherine Canal. Wreaths on the site of Alexander II's murder

Token struck in honour of the silver wedding of Alexander II and Maria Alexandrovna. St Petersburg, Russia. 1866. SM "Peterhof"

Caché with the monogram of Empress Maria Alexandrovna. Russia. 1850s – 1880s. SM "Peterhof'

C. Schultz from a photograph by A. Denier. *Portrait of Empress Maria Alexandrovna.* 1850s–1880s. SM "Peterhof"

Maria Alexandrovna, née Princess Marie of Hesse-Darmstadt (1824–1880), consort of Emperor Alexander II

Emperor Alexander II with his sons Nikolai, Alexander, Vladimir, Alexei, Sergei and his daughter Maria

The children of Alexander Maria were educated for a long time together with Nicholas I's younger children. Both families spent the summer in the Cottage Palace, where Nicholas with pleasure taught both his sons and grandsons. Altogether Maria gave birth to eight children and one daughter. The first child, Alexander, who was born in 1842, died in 1949 to a great sorrow of his parents. In 1743 Nikolai was born, who was the heir to the throne until his death in 1865. The next one was Alexander (the future Emperor) followed by his younger brothers Vladimir (1847–1909), Alexei (1850–1908), Sergei (1857–1905) and Pavel (1860–1918). The only daughter, Maria, was born in 1853 and died in 1920.

Alexander II's private life was complicated by his love affair. In 1841 he married Maria Alexandrovna (the Princess Maximiliane Wilhelmine Auguste Sophie Marie of Darmstadt), an unusually meek and kind, but fragile and sick woman. Over the years the Tsar began to keep apart from his wife. In 1866 his romance with the nineteen-year-old Princess Yekaterina Dolgorukaya began. In 1872 she gave him the first child named Georgy. Alexander loved Princess Dolgorukaya very much and was attached to her; he even settled her in the Winter Palace, although his wife was alive. Princess Dolgorukaya bore to him two more children, the daughters Olga and Yekaterina. Alexander II issued a decree granting them nobility and the princely title with the name of Yuryevsky. Empress Maria Alexandrovna died in May 1880 and soon Princess Yuryevskaya and Alexander II had a secret wedding in the Tsarskoye Selo Palace. From this moment the Tsar did not hide his happiness from his entourage any more, however, he was destined to live on less than a year…

The Most Illustrious Princess Yekaterina Yuryevskaya with her son Georgy and her daughter Olga. 1880s. SA RF

After the death of her husband Yekaterina Yuryevskaya retained her apartments in the Winter Palace, but later went abroad and settled at the Cote d'Azure in France. She died at Nice in 1922.

I. Chevalier from a drawing by I. Yegorov. *Portrait of Emperor Alexander II and Tsesarevich Nikolai Alexandrovich.* 1855. SM "Peterhof"

Plate from a service with the coat of arms of Alexander II and Princess Yuryevskaya. Paris, France. 1880. SM "Peterhof"

ALEXANDER III

Alexander Alexandrovich
(26 February 1845, St Petersburg – 20 October 1894, Livadia, the Crimea),
the Tsar from 1 March 1881

After the death of Alexander II his elder son Alexander succeeded the throne. On the day of his father's murder Alexander III left the Winter Palace and concealed himself at Gatchina that became his abode for many years. The Tsar was afraid of attempts upon his life that made the state of his family a nightmare from the middle of the 1860s. Owing to the same reason he postponed his coronation to be held in Moscow for two and a half years. At the doors of the "Gatchina prisoner", as the Tsar was called in society, there were guards throughout the day. On 11 March 1881 Alexander's tutor, Konstantin Pobedonostsev, wrote to his pupil that he should personally shut the doors before going to bed "not only in the bedroom, but in all subsequent rooms, including the entrance door." Admittedly, Alexander III had every reason to take protective measures in the 1880s – the terrorists of the People's Will organization prepared no less than five attempts upon his life.

The Emperor was, as Sergei Witte wrote, a man of "quite a usual mind", but remarkable and expressive in his own way. The Emperor "was not pretty and rather bear-like in his manners", he looked like "a large Russian *moujik* from central provinces… and nevertheless his appearance in which his im-

P. Zabolotsky. *Portrait of Emperor Alexander III.*
1889. SM "Peterhof"

S. Zarianko. *Portrait of Grand Duke Alexander Alexandrovich*. 1867. SM "Peterhof"

Tutor of Alexander III,
Chief Procurator of the Holy Synod
Konstantin Pobedonostsev
(1827–1907)

mense character was reflected, as well as beautiful heart, placidity, justice and at the same time hardness, undoubtedly impresses people around him."

From his early years he was an opponent of reforms in the Western manner and an enemy of every kind of establishments that could change the autocratic regime. The terrible events of 1 March 1881 shattered Alexander III and made it impossible for him a further movement along the path of reforms. On his accession he dismissed all the liberal ministers of his father with Loris-Melikov at their head.

After Alexander III had ascended the throne, the police-state regime in the country intensified. With the help of provocations and the introduction of agents into revolutionary organizations the authorities managed to cope with the so-called "bomb-throwers" of the People's Will terrorist organization.

View of the Gatchina Palace from the station

The Heir Tsesarevich and Grand Duke Alexander Alexandrovich with his consort Tsesarevna Maria Fiodorovna. Late 1860s. SA RF

Notice about the Holy Coronation of Emperor Alexander III and Empress Maria Fiodorovna. 1883. SM "Peterhof"

The Coronation Ceremony in Moscow. Emperor Alexander III and Empress Maria Fiodorovna on the Red Porch. 1883. SA RF

Journalist Mikhail
Katkov (1818–1887)

In the reign of Alexander III the so-called age of "popular autocracy" began, which was largely introduced to overcome the western trend of Alexander II's policies. Mikhail Katkov, the publisher of the newspaper *Moskovskiye Vedomosti*, became an energetic champion of the ideas of "popular, original, warm autocracy" linked with the people by the "vivid link" of the gentry. It was also he who wrote the project for the Manifesto of 29 April 1881 known as the "*ananas* [pineapple] manifesto" – a pun on words because of its high-flown style. That Manifesto was the first step in an attack of the reforms undertaken by Alexander II and of any, even moderate, liberalism. The uniform of the Russian army was accordingly changed or "russified". Instead of an elegant European half-caftans, the Russian troops were to wear wide Oriental trousers, coloured sashes and lamb fur hats that suited Alexander III himself. As one officer put it, it was the *moujik's* uniform. The establishment of the regime of "popular autocracy" led to the intensified Russification on the outskirts and the stirring up of Russian nationalism. The essence of the economic policy of Alexander III's government was in the revision of the reforms of the 1860s and in working out the economic doctrine of "popular autocracy" based on the strengthening of the power of the state in all spheres, a control of the activities of the *zemstvo* and other elected bodies. The authorities strove to regulate the economic life of the country: bread tariffs, bank activities, duties and customs; they began to buy railways to the state.

The first Grand
Entrée of Emperor
Alexander III

Coronation rouble. The Mint, St Petersburg.
1883. SM "Peterhof"

Menu of the dinner organized in honour of the Holy
Coronation of Emperor Alexander III and Empress
Maria Fiodorovna. 24 May 1883. SA RF

Throne armchair of Empress
Maria Fiodorovna.
St Petersburg, Russia. 1883.
SM "Peterhof"

The Coronation of Emperor Alexander III.
From *The Coronation Book*. 1883. SM "Peterhof"

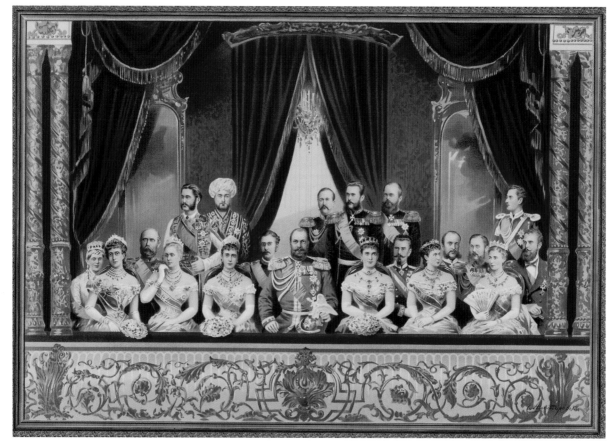

Festive performance in the Bolshoi Theatre on 18 May 1883. From the album *The Holy Coronation of the Sovereign Emperor Alexander III*. 1883

Admittedly, Alexander III himself was not a warlike and cruel man – his reign passed without wars. Russia evaded a participation in any conflicts that disturbed Europe in those years. A search for allies was Russia's main problem. At first it placed great hopes on a friendship with Germany. But the efforts failed owing to trade rivalry of the two countries and Germany's unfriendly position on the Balkans, where it had a closer ally, Austria-Hungary. Therefore Russia began to seek rapprochement with republican France that was interested in forming an anti-German union. In 1891 Alexander III had to listen to the *Marseillaise* hated by all monarchs and monarchists – a French squadron came to Kronstadt with a visit of friendship, where the Russian Tsar met it in a solemn atmosphere. The union with France became the basis of Russia's foreign policy for many years. It was useful for France, too – Russia twice succeeded in restraining Germany from attacking France. A monument to the Franco-Russian Union concluded in 1893 is the Alexander III Bridge then opened in Paris.

Device of a lady-in-waiting with the monogram of Empress Maria Fiodorovna. St Petersburg, Russia. 1885–94. SM "Peterhof"

Paper-weight for a desk. C. Fabergé Company. 1880s. From the Study of Maria Fiodorovna in the Cottage Palace. SM "Peterhof"

Empress Maria Fiodorovna, née Princess Sophie Friedericke Dagmar of Denmark (1847–1928), consort of Emperor Alexander III

K. Brozh. *Ball in the St Nicholas Hall of the Winter Palace*. Late 1880s

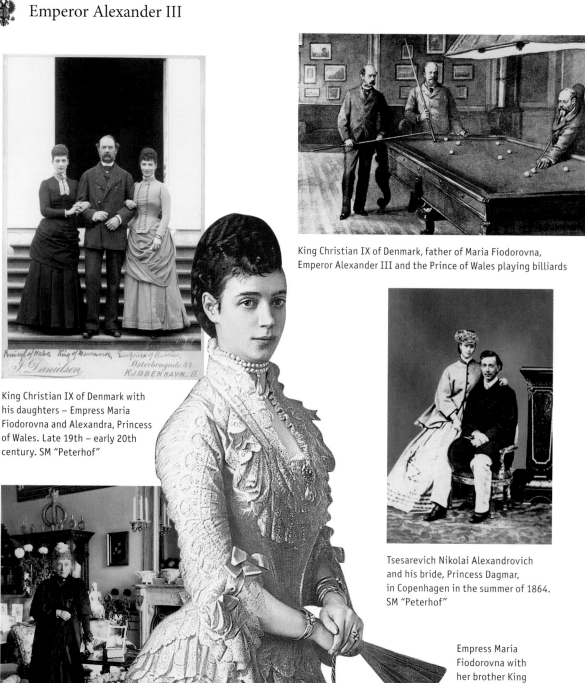

King Christian IX of Denmark, father of Maria Fiodorovna,
Emperor Alexander III and the Prince of Wales playing billiards

King Christian IX of Denmark with
his daughters – Empress Maria
Fiodorovna and Alexandra, Princess
of Wales. Late 19th – early 20th
century. SM "Peterhof"

Tsesarevich Nikolai Alexandrovich
and his bride, Princess Dagmar,
in Copenhagen in the summer of 1864.
SM "Peterhof"

Empress Maria
Fiodorovna with
her brother King
George I of Greece.
Late 1880s. SA RF

Louise, Queen
of Denmark. 1890s.
SA RF

Empress
Maria
Fiodorovna

The family of Emperor Alexander III. 1888. SA RF

In the first row, left to right: Grand Duke Mikhail, Emperor Alexander III, Grand Duchess Olga,
Grand Duke Georgy; in the second row: Empress Maria Fiodorovna, Heir Tsesarevich Nikolai Alexandrovich,
Grand Duchess Xenia Alexandrovna.

Emperor Alexander III with his family in Livadia. 1893. SA RF

Alexander III and Empress Maria Fiodorovna had an amicable family. She, a young Danish princess (Sophie Friederike Dagmar before her conversion to Orthodoxy), had been at first the bride of the then heir to the throne Tsesarevich Nicholas Alexandrovich, the elder son of Alexander II. However,

Writing set of Emperor Alexander III. The Palace of Peter I, Strelna. SM "Peterhof"

the twenty-two-year-old Nicholas fell sick before their wedding and died. His death was met with general regret – the successor was a clever, well-educated and kind young man. Two years later, in 1867, Dagmar agreed to marry the younger brother of the deceased Nicholas, Alexander, who liked her very much.

Maria Fiodorovna was a beautiful, clever, merry woman. She bore six children and rarely parted with Alexander – they even went bear – hunting together. Later, having lost her husband, she failed to reach an understanding with the wife of his son Nicholas II and lived alone. In 1919 Maria Fiodorovna was carried away from the Crimea and she died in Denmark, her native land, in 1928.

Alexander III enjoyed life. He was a passionate fisher and hunter. His word was a final decision for all grown up members of the Romanov family. They knew that the Tsar was intolerant to any "liberties" and conjugal infidelity

Medal struck in honour of
the miraculous rescue of
the royal family.
1888. SM "Peterhof"

On 17 October 1888,
at the Borki Station
45 miles from Kharkov
there occurred a railway
catastrophe: the royal train
derailed for technical reasons. Nearly 50 people
were wounded and killed. The royal family was
in the carriage that served as a dining room and
it was only thanks to its roof, which coiled like
a sphere, that the Tsar and his family remained
alive. A legend arose at once about the mighty
Tsar who supported the falling roof over his wife
and children. This lucky chance was perceived in
the royal family as a sign from above that nothing would happen with the Romanovs.

The crush of the royal train at the Borki Station
on 17 October 1888. SA RF

among his relations because he believed that the first family of Russia should
be a model of truly Christian conduct for the subjects. That is why he strictly
condemned his father for his love affair with Yurovskaya.

The Emperor, despite his powerful appearance, did not have strong
health. He died in October 1894 from kidney disease still under fifty, at
Livadia, his favourite place in the Crimea. Alexander II died quietly, encircled by his loving children and wife, and sure that he had fulfilled his
principal mission on the earth – he saved Russia from upheavals. It was
indeed so: his unbending will and purposefullness have largely contributed to his success. It is not a mere coincidence that when Sergei Witte
was asked in 1907, "How to save Russia?", he pointed to the portrait of
Alexander II and said: "Resurrect him!"

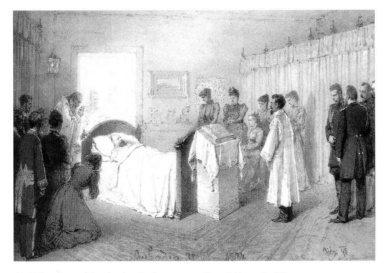

M. Zichy. *Funeral Service for the Commemoration of Alexander III
in His Bedroom in the Livadia Palace*. 1895

NICHOLAS II

Nikolai Alexandrovich
(6 May 1868, St Petersburg – 17 July 1918, Yekaterinburg),
the Tsar from 20 October 1894 to 1 March 1917

The reign of Nicholas II divides into two stages – before and after the revolution of 1905. In the first period Nicholas, hostile to any liberal tendencies, tried to evade imminent political reforms relying on the strength of the autocratic tradition. The awful defeat in the Russo-Japanese War of 1904–05 and the revolution of 1905, however, forced him to make political concessions, but he regarded them as temporary measures and therefore hindered in all ways the development of parliamentarism in Russia. Towards the end of his reign he lost the support of all layers of society and the majority of population in Russia welcomed his overthrowing. The start of Nicholas II's reign was marked not only by the colourful coronation ceremony held on 14 May 1896 in Moscow, but a terrible stampede on the Khodynka Field during the coronation. The Tsar learned about the catastrophe in the morning, but did not cancel any of the forthcoming festivities and in the evening opened the ball with the charming wife of the French ambassador Montebello… And although later the Tsar would pay visits to hospitals and donate money to the families of those who perished in the Khodynka stampede, it was too late – an indifference to his people demonstrated by the Tsar during the first

N. Schilder. *Portrait of Emperor Nicholas II.*
Late 19th century. SM "Peterhof"

V. Serov. *The Anointment of Emperor Nicholas II*. 1897. From *The Coronation Book of Nicholas II*. SM "Peterhof"

hours of the catastrophe would cost him dear. It was after this accident that he became nicknamed "Nicholas the Bloody". Nicholas II had good education, he loved art and literature. But he lacked the will, resolution and sincerity of his father. Nicholas II was thought to be deceitful, secretive and indifferent to people. He did not posses unusual powers of mind to become an outstanding politician.

In 1894 he married a woman he loved. Empress Alexandra Fiodorovna was the Princess Victoria Alice Helen Louise Beatrice of Hesse-Darmstadt before her conversion to Orthodoxy (she was called Alix at home). They formed a strikingly harmonious couple and lived in accord and love for many years. The Empress was shy; she did not like society and avoided contacts with those around her. Proud and reticent, she failed to win the favour either of high society or of the people and that factor was harmful to the regime in the eyes of the general public. Her world was confined to the family and at that she had a strong influence on Nicholas II, not always useful for the state. Alexandra Fiodorovna became a zealous Orthodox believer, but like many neophytes, she was inclined to mysticism and deeply believed in miracles, which could be easily explained by

Minister of the Interior
Viacheslav Plehve
(1846–1904)

Ballerina Mathilde Kschessinska

Alexander III, Nicholas II's father, was intolerable to adulteries in his family. He reprimanded his father for that, was critical of his uncle Konstantin, who had a liaison with a ballerina. Dancers often became favourites of the grand dukes – such was a whimsical fashion of the period. The future Emperor Nicholas II also paid tribute to this "family" passion of the Romanovs to ballerinas. Before his marriage to Alice he became seriously captivated by Mathilde Kschessinska – the prima dancer of the Mariinsky. He was not resolute enough to conflict with his father and marry her, but he continued his liaison with Mathilde until 1894. After a break with her lover, Mathilde became enamoured with Grand Duke Sergei Mikhailovich and later with Grand Duke Andrei Vladimirovich; she gave birth to a son, Vladimir, by the latter. She died in France in 1971.

Tsesarevich Nikolai Alexandrovich with his bride Princess Alice of Hesse

her desire to deliver her only and beloved son and successor Tsesarevich Alexei from a terrible disease – hemophilia.

For a long time the most prominent figure in interior affairs was Sergei Witte, the Minister of Finance. He actively supported the policy of attracting foreign capitals to Russia. In 1895–97 gold circulation was introduced in Russia according to Witte's project. Witte combined this policy with the protection of the Russian industry and trade. In 1902 Viacheslav Plehve, the Minister of Internal Affairs, grew into a no less influential figure for Nicholas II. Plehve was the experienced chief of police and a clever politician capable for a compromise. He believed that reforms were necessary for Russia and that "the very methods used by the government were obsolete", but that it was necessary to carry out the reforms under

Two cousins – Emperor Nicholas II of Russia and King George V of England. 1910s. SA RF

Empress Alexandra Fiodorovna with Grand Princess Olga Nikolayevna, Emperor Nicholas II, Victoria, Queen of Great Britain, and Edward, Prince of Wales. London. 1896. SA RF

Grand Duke Sergei Alexandrovich (1857–1905), the fifth son of Emperor Alexander II

Grand Duchess Yelizaveta Fiodorovna, née Princess of Hesse-Darmstadt (1864–1918), from 1884 – consort of Grand Duke Sergei Alexandrovich

the auspices of the autocracy. In 1904 Plehve was killed by terrorists of the Socialist-Revolutionary group led by Yevno Azef.

Thanks to the marriage of Nicholas to Alix, the Romanovs became related to the English royal house and to the Hohenzollern dynasty. Queen Victoria (1837–1901) had nine children in marriage to Prince-Consort Albert. Their elder daughter Victoria was given in marriage to the German Emperor Frederick III. She gave him a son, Victoria's grandson, who would become Emperor William II. The brother of the younger Victoria, Prince Edward, who ascended the English throne after the death of Queen Victoria as Edward VII (1901–1910), was in marriage to Princess Alexandra of Denmark, sister of Princess Dagmar or the Russian Empress Maria Fiodorovna. Alexandra gave birth to a son, George, the future King George V of England (1910–1936). Being Nicholas II's cousin, George had a strong resemblance

Members of the imperial family. Tsarskoye Selo. Late 1890s. CAPhD

to the Emperor of Russia. The English and Russian dynasties were linked by another blood relationship, too. Princess Alice, the second daughter of Queen Victoria, married Grand Duke Ludwig IV of Hessen. She had three daughters, Elizabeth, Irene and Alice. The elder granddaughter of Queen Victoria, Elizabeth (born in 1864 and known as Yelizaveta Fiodorovna on conversion to Orthodoxy) married Grand Duke Sergei Alexandrovich, son of Alexander II. It was her younger sister Alice who married Nicholas II and became Empress Alexandra Fiodorovna. In 1905 Sergei Alexandrovich was killed by the terrorist Ivan Kaliayev right in his study in Moscow.

The family of Nicholas and Alexandra was unusually amicable. It was cemented by a deep feeling of Nicholas and Alexandra to each other. Then children began to appear, at first all were girls: Olga (1895), Tatyana (1897), Maria (1899) and Anastasia (1901). The parents were happy, but there was also a reason for a distress – the Sovereign needed a successor. At last on 30 July 1904 a long-awaited boy, Alexei, was born in Alexandria. The parents' love to their son grew hysterical and painful when it turned out that Alexei had an incurable disease – hemophilia. After that the royal family came to be influenced by the Siberian "starets" Grigory Rasputin, who had an unusual ability to arrest Tsesarevich Alexei's bleeding caused by hemophilia. The Empress immoderately trusted him and thought him to be a saint. And Rasputin, profiting by his position, intruded in policy, which caused general irritation in society. A conspiracy was organized against the favourite; Rasputin was invited to the palace of Prince Yusupov and killed there.

Emperor Nicholas II and his family. 1904. SA RF

Grigory Rasputin (real surname Novykh) (1872–1916) and Varnava, Archbishop of Siberia. 1910s. SA RF

Nicholas II visiting the troops leaving for the front during the Russo-Japanese War. 1904. CAPhD

The war against Japan in 1904–05 became a dark period of the reign of Nicholas II. It was caused by the sharpening disagreements between Russia and Japan competing for the spheres of influence at the Far East. Japan prepared for that war better than Russia. The Russian army and fleet suffered several bitter failures, and Tsushima, associated with the defeat of the Russian fleet sent all the way from the Baltic Sea, became a common name for designating military catastrophes. Instead of uniting society as a result of a "small victorious war over the small Asians", Russia received thousands of killed soldiers, an economic devastation, a humiliated national dignity and, eventually, a revolution.

The defence of the Port-Arthur fortress became the crucial event of the war. The Russian army, defeated several times in Manchuria, was retreating farther away from the fortress. On 14–15 May after the fleet had perished in the Battle of Tsushima, the position of the Port Arthur garrison became hopeless and it surrendered. The Treaty of Portsmouth signed by Sergei Witte with the Japanese in 1905 did not bring a relief to Russia – the country was already in a grip of revolution.

Mobilized soldiers report for duty at the barracks. 1904. CAPhD

The defence of Port Arthur. Fire over the Golden Mountain

Port Arthur. View of the "High Mountain" from the "New Battery". 1904–05. CAPhD

Peterhof. Emperor Nicholas II with an icon of Christ
the Saviour addresses the 148th Infantry Caspian regiment
before its departure for the theatre of operations in
Manchuria. 16 July 1904. CAPhD

Russian infantry in Manchuria. [1904–05]. SA RF

The beginning of the revolutionary events is usually taken to be 9 January 1905, when workers on strike went to the Tsar with a petition. The petition was not accepted and the troops opened fire at the demonstrators. Several hundred people died from bullets. "Bloody Sunday" caused large-scale strikes, revolts and mutinies in the army and fleet and all that forced the Tsar to bring the retired Witte back to power. Witte drew up the October Manifesto that granted freedom to the people and announced elections to the State Duma. 17 October 1905 was a crucial date in the history of Russia. On that day Nicholas recorded in his diary: "17th October. Monday. The anniversary of the catastrophe

St Petersburg. Soldiers near the Narva Gate. 9 January 1905. CAPhD

Session of the First State Duma. April 1906. CAPhD

I. Repin. *17 October 1905*. 1911

Ceremony of the inauguration of the State Duma and
the State Council in the Throne Room of the Winter Palace.
27 April 1906. SA RF

Minister of Finance Sergei Witte
(1894–1915). 1904. SA RF

[at Borki]. I signed the Manifesto at 5
p.m. After such a day my head became
heavy and my thoughts got confused.
My God, help us, calm Russia." Notably, Grand Duke Nikolai Nikolayevich,
the eldest in the Romanov family, on
the tense days of 1905, in breach of
his oath, took a tremendously daring
and important decision: he forbade
all officers, members of the Romanov
family, to participate in the suppression of popular disturbances.

Prime Minister Piotr Stolypin
(1862–1911)

Session of the 2nd State Duma.
1907. CAPhD

Between 1906 and 1911 the Russian interior policy was determined by the strong-willed and resolute Piotr Stolypin (born 1862), who was appointed the head of the government. He had to fight against revolutionaries and peasant mutinies and at the same time to carry out reforms. The Prime Minister thought his agrarian reform to be the principle vehicle of improvement. He published as parts of this reform the laws on the dissolution of village communities and on the right of peasants to have their own farms. To assist the peasants leaving the community, the Peasant Bank was transformed and other measures of encouragement were worked out. Stolypin set as his task to create, within twenty years, the estate of wealthy peasants-proprietors.

Stolypin had strained relations with the State Duma. On 3 June 1907 he dissolved the Second Duma that was too liberal for him. That

Palace Embankment. 1910s. CAPhD

measure was regarded as a coup. Stolypin changed the franchise so that the conservative parties co-operating with Stolypin received the majority in the Third Duma. However, the Tsar and the court clique that desired no reforms at all disliked the authoritarian Stolypin. On 1 September 1911 Stolypin was mortally wounded at the theatre in Kiev by the Socialist-revolutionary Dmitry Bogrov, who, strange as it may seem, appeared with a revolver in the carefully guarded theatre. With Stolypin's death Russia lost its last chances to renovate avoiding the horrors of revolution.

Emperor Nicholas II
and the Heir Tsesarevich
Alexei Nikolayevich

Towards 1913 the economy of the country was on the rise and many people believed that after so many years of unrest there arrived an era of prosperity and the Russian "Silver Age" in culture. By 1913 the financial reform carried out by Sergei Witte had fully justified itself. One rouble became equal to 2.16 German marks, 2.67 franks and 2.54 Austro-Hungarian crowns. The tercentenary of the Romanov House was celebrated in that year. The three centuries of Russian history from Tsar Mikhail Fiodorovich to Nicholas II were described in the official circles as an incessant chain of victories and outstanding accomplishments. Luxurious festivities and grand balls were held one after another. But these festivals turned out to have been the last in the history of the Russian Empire.

Muscovites waiting for the arrival of Emperor Nicholas II during the celebration of the 300th Anniversary of the Romanov House. Moscow. 1913. CAPhD

Nicholas II receiving bread-and-salt on the day of his arrival for the celebration of the 300th Anniversary of the Romanov House. Yaroslavl. 1913. CAPhD

Empress Alexandra Fiodorovna with the Heir Tsesarevich Alexei in a chariot on Red Square during the celebration of the 300th Anniversary of the Romanov House. Moscow. 1913. CAPhD

Emperor Nicholas II,
Empress Alexandra
Fiodorovna and
Tsesarevich Alexei (in
the arms of his usher)
during the celebration
of the 300th Anniversary
of the Romanov House.
Moscow. 1913. CAPhD

Ceremony of
the foundation of a
monument to Minin
and Pozharsky in
the presence of Emperor
Nicholas II and members
of his family during
the celebration of
the 300th Anniversary
of the Romanov House.
Nizhni Novgorod. 1913.
CAPhD

Participants in the manifestation at the corner of Nevsky Prospekt and Mikhailovskaya Street on the occasion of the rejection of the Serbian Ultimatum to Austria-Hungary. 28 July 1914. CAPhD

On 1 August 1914 Germany declared war on Russia. The whole country enjoyed the period of general unity in those days. On 2 August 1914 crowds of people initiated a demonstration that marched to Palace Square to express their support of the Tsar. As a result of the growth of anti-German moods the capital was renamed Petrograd instead of St Petersburg.

Memorial postcard "Reign for the enemy's fear". 1914. SM "Peterhof"

Emperor Nicholas II going around the motor unit of the training automobile company before their departure for the front. The Semionovsky Parade Grounds, Petrograd. 1914. CAPhD

Emperor Nicholas II, a Catholic priest and the suite in the area of combat operations.
1915. CAPhD

Soldiers at tactical training in gas-masks. The army in the field.
1915–17. CAPhD

The mobilization encompassed about 10,000,000 people, and practically there were no more strikes. The attack at the front, successful at the beginning, ended in a defeat of the million-strong Russian army in Eastern Prussia at Tannenberg. This defeat was partly compensated by the successes at the Austrian direction, where the Russian army succeeded to occupy a half of Austrian Galicia. The counteroffensive of the Austro-German armies in May 1915 ended in Russia's crushing defeat – it had to cede Lithuania, Galicia and Poland to the enemy. A half of the army was put out of action. The economic situation in the country began to aggravate rapidly and the production of ammunition failed to meet the demands of the front. A lack of talented commanders, thefts in the rear and senseless victims increasingly irritated society.

In the autumn of 1915 Nicholas II, who had no military talent, displaced the Commander-in-Chief Grand Duke Nikolai Nikolayevich, popular in the army, and took the command himself. That was a serious error – from that moment all military failures were ascribed to the Tsar himself. Only once under his command the Russian troops led by General Brusilov made a successful breakthrough in the Austrian front, but soon this attack began to exhaust due to a lack of ammunition. The results of the military activities in 1916 and early 1917 proved to be highly depressing. The enemy at the German front was held in check with difficulty. The army lacked indispensable things,

Cavalry General Alexei Brusilov (1853–1926)

soldiers were freezing in trenches, the number of deserters increased and anti-military moods were growing in the rear. In the course of the war Russia's lag in the production of up-to-date military equipment became particularly obvious. The army felt a keen shortage of airplanes, cars and trucks, and there were very few tanks. Horses remained the principal tractive force as before. People blamed for all these failures the Empress, a German, who allegedly surrounded herself with German spies and who suppressed Nicholas's will. Although there were no spies near Alexandra Fiodorovna, her influence upon her husband proved really to be enormous and in general negative.

The army in the field. 1915. CAPhD

Tsesarevich Alexei with his
teachers Gillard, Voeykov,
Gibbs and Petrov in
the General Staff.
1916. CAPhD

The Council of Ministers. The Tsar's Staff at the Baranovichi Station. 1915. CAPhD

In 1916 a crisis in society was under way. The military production began to destroy the interior market. There was a previously unseen shortage of industrial products in Russia; prices for all goods went up. The standards of living in cities and towns rapidly impaired. Queues for bread became a scaring symbol of the impending catastrophe. The authorities failed to overcome the inflation raise of prices, corruption and stealing. The saving idea of ration cards was realized only in 1917. At the beginning of 1917 moods in the army grew especially dangerous for the government. Agitators of various revolutionary parties, who called soldiers not to obey and to rebel, were active in the troops. The difficult conditions of life in trenches and a feeling that the war is senseless, enhanced by rumours about all-round treason, increasingly seized the soldiers, yesterday's peasants. The garrisons of large cities were especially disposed to rebellious moods. They were easily impressed by revolutionary propaganda because they would not like to go to the front.

Petrograd. Demonstration of soldiers on Nevsky Prospekt. 1917. CAPhD

Empress Alexandra Fiodorovna and Tsesarevich Alexei riding around the troops before the parade of the Guard Reserve Battalions on the Field of Mars. Petrograd. 1916. CAPhD

A group of officers and soldiers with their relations at the station before their departure to the army in the field. Petrograd. 1916. CAPhD

Petrograd. Manifestation for peace. 1917. CAPhD

Grand Duke Mikhail Alexandrovich
(1878–1918), brother of Emperor Nicholas II

Act of abdication of Emperor Nicholas II.
2 March 1917. SA RF

Act of abdication of Grand Duke Mikhail
Alexandrovich. 3 March 1917. SA RF

On 26 and 27 February 1917 a mutiny of soldiers in the barracks of the St Petersburg garrison began. The rebellious soldiers started to fraternize with demonstrating workers. Then the rebels captured the Arsenal and gave 40,000 rifles to the crowd. The authorities were powerless to resist their armed onslaught. The people demanded to overthrow the monarchy and to proclaim a republic. On 27 February the "Special Committee" of the State Duma, after a meeting with the Petrograd Soviet formed by the newly formed leftist parties, established a new government headed by Prince Georgy Lvov. It demanded Nicholas II to abdicate in favour of his brother, Grand Duke Mikhail Alexandrovich.

The Emperor ceased to resist only after he had received telegrams of similar content from all the front commanders. He abdicated on 2 March 1917 in favour of Grand Duke Mikhail Alexandrovich.

Although Alexander III loved his youngest son Mikhail best, while dying he did not want to change the law of succession and his eldest son Nicholas came to the throne after him. Grand Duke Mikhail was considered the heir until the birth of a son to Nicholas II, Alexei, in 1904, but after that he gladly gave up the title of the Tsesarevich. Grand Duke Mikhail Alexandrovich was a simple, easy-going, merry man, interested in music. Strong and brave, he nevertheless had a meek and even weak character. He had grave relations with his brother, the Emperor, and his mother, Dowager Empress Maria Fiodorovna, because he married, against their will, the twice-divorced Natalia Sheremetevskaya, the most irresistible beauty of St Petersburg. To evade the anger of his regal relatives, he had to live abroad for several years. With the outbreak of the First World War Mikhail was appointed a division commander. On 3 March 1917 Mikhail, hiding at a private apartment, received a delegation of political figures. On seeing, however, that they had different views on the future and did not guarantee his safety, he denied "to take the supreme power" after formally being the Emperor only for a day, on 3 March 1917. Thus Russia ceased to be a monarchy. The last Emperor Michael II (Mikhail Alexandrovich) was arrested in Gatchina and exiled to Perm, where on 13 July 1918 he was taken out to a forest and shot by the Bolsheviks.

Nikolai Alexandrovich Romanov with his son Alexei. Tobolsk. 1918. SA RF

Arrested on 8 March 1917, Nicholas II was kept in the Alexander Palace at Tsarskoye Selo together with his family (his wife, their son and their daughters) until July 1917. Then they were transferred to Tobolsk and later, at the end of May 1918, to Ekaterinburg. There, on orders from the Kremlin, they were ferociously killed in the basement of the merchant Ipatyev's mansion by the secret police and stealthily buried in the forest. The remains of the Tsar and his relations found near Yekaterinburg were identified in 1998 and reburied in the Cathedral of SS Peter and Paul in St Petersburg.

The SS Peter and Paul Cathedral. Tomb of the last Russian Emperor Nicholas II and his family

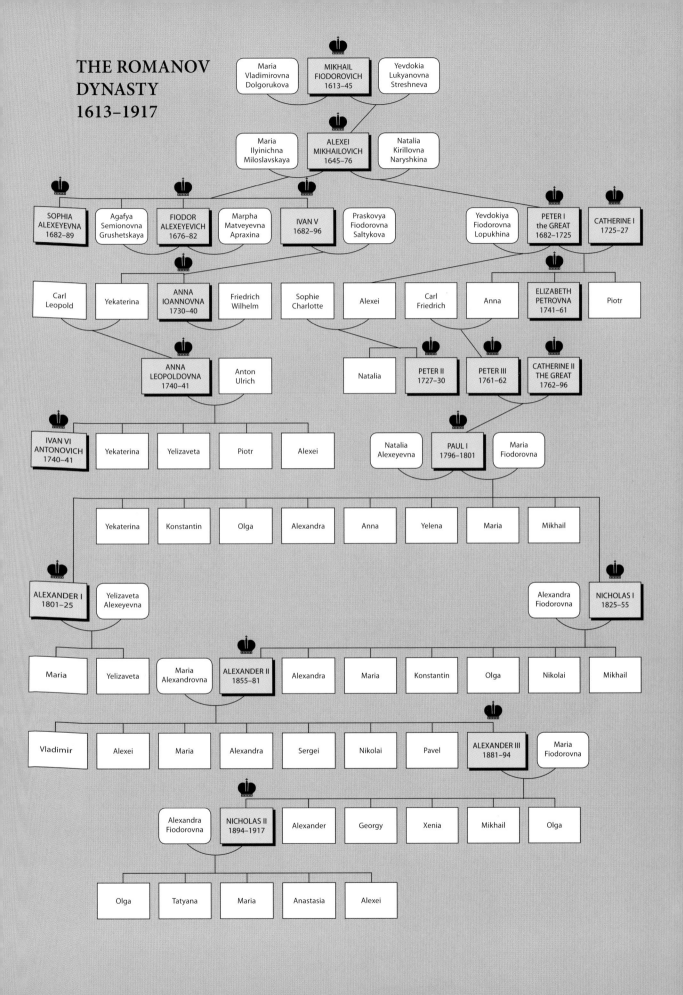

THE ROMANOV DYNASTY 1613–1917

Maria Vladimirovna Dolgorukova — MIKHAIL FIODOROVICH 1613–45 — Yevdokia Lukyanovna Streshneva

Maria Ilyinichna Miloslavskaya — ALEXEI MIKHAILOVICH 1645–76 — Natalia Kirillovna Naryshkina

SOPHIA ALEXEYEVNA 1682–89 · Agafya Semionovna Grushetskaya — FIODOR ALEXEYEVICH 1676–82 — Marpha Matveyevna Apraxina · IVAN V 1682–96 — Praskovya Fiodorovna Saltykova · Yevdokiya Fiodorovna Lopukhina — PETER I the GREAT 1682–1725 — CATHERINE I 1725–27

Carl Leopold — Yekaterina · ANNA IOANNOVNA 1730–40 — Friedrich Wilhelm · Sophie Charlotte — Alexei · Carl Friedrich — Anna · ELIZABETH PETROVNA 1741–61 · Piotr

ANNA LEOPOLDOVNA 1740–41 — Anton Ulrich · Natalia · PETER II 1727–30 · PETER III 1761–62 — CATHERINE II THE GREAT 1762–96

IVAN VI ANTONOVICH 1740–41 · Yekaterina · Yelizaveta · Piotr · Alexei · Natalia Alexeyevna — PAUL I 1796–1801 — Maria Fiodorovna

Yekaterina · Konstantin · Olga · Alexandra · Anna · Yelena · Maria · Mikhail

ALEXANDER I 1801–25 — Yelizaveta Alexeyevna · Alexandra Fiodorovna — NICHOLAS I 1825–55

Maria · Yelizaveta · Maria Alexandrovna — ALEXANDER II 1855–81 · Alexandra · Maria · Konstantin · Olga · Nikolai · Mikhail

Vladimir · Alexei · Maria · Alexandra · Sergei · Nikolai · Pavel · ALEXANDER III 1881–94 — Maria Fiodorovna

Alexandra Fiodorovna — NICHOLAS II 1894–1917 · Alexander · Georgy · Xenia · Mikhail · Olga

Olga · Tatyana · Maria · Anastasia · Alexei

Contents

Text by
Yevgeny Anisimov

Scientific Editor
Nina Vernova

Heads of the Project
Vadim Znamenov,
General Director of the State
Museum-Preserve "Peterhof",
and Liubov Pantina,
Director of Abris Art
Publishers

Compiled by
Anna Barkhatova

Edited by
Ana Barkhatova and Tatyana
Burkova

Translated from the Russian
by Valery Fateyev

Design and layout by
Sergei Plaxin

Technical treatment of
materials by
Sergei Plaxin and Alexei
Yarilov

In the book are used materials
from the collections of the State
Museum-Preserves of Peterhof
and Pavlovsk (SM "Peterhof",
SM "Pavlovsk"), the State
Hermitage, the State Russian
Museum, the State Archive of the
Russian Federation (SA RF), the
Central State Archive of Cinema
and Photo Documents (CAPhD),
the Moscow Kremlin, the State
Tretyakov Gallery and other
Russian and foreign museums.

Almanac: "Treasures of Russia"
Issue 76

ISBN 978-5-88810-076-9

Printed and bound in
"Premium Press"

Тираж 1000. Цена договорная
№ П 2462 в СЗРУ Госкомпечати
РФ от 30.04.97

© Abris Art Publishers,
St Petersburg, Peterhof 2007